Maranatha **Awakenings**

Inspired poems to aid in understanding the truth for this time, gaining victory over sin, and enduring until the end.

SAMARA FLEMING

Ph.D.

PRINTED IN
THE UNITED STATES OF AMERICA

Edited Edition.

Third printing.

Cover Design by Samara Fleming.

Copyright © 2022

ISBN: 978-0-578-27014-2

Simple Preparations Publishing
Macclesfield, North Carolina

Dedication

I dedicate this book of rhyme

To those who would know the time

And would examine their heart

For that's where to start

To give God their heart, soul, and mind.

Acknowledgments

I truly thank everyone who has ever encouraged me to write a book of godly poetry, especially the members of my family.

I would especially like to thank Mika, Hil, and Maria for all of their invaluable contributions, which made this work worthy of, and fit for, publication. Special thanks also to Denny and Deanna for their thoughtful contributions in making this work a reality.

Tremendous gratitude, praise, and thankfulness go to God for His abundant love and inspiration when writing the poems contained within this book. I also thank Him for using Mr. Robinette to provide the experience I needed to reach this goal. Mr. Robinette: Thank you, sir! I am also grateful for the talented Christian poets who inspired me to again pick up my pen and write for the Lord!

Table of Contents

A Call to Action: Talents

When God puts something on your heart to do, never let worldly qualifications keep you from doing it. I am living proof that if God gives you a burden to do something, He will provide the way and the means for you to do it in His timing. All talents are from the Lord. He qualifies the talent He gives you. You can rest assured that He will give you the knowledge, wisdom, and skill to make your work for Him a success, and He will align all the ways to move forward in what He would have you to do.

God-given Gifts!

All of us are born with at least one innate ability, at least one talent, or gift. In this book, I use the words *abilities, talents,* and *gifts* interchangeably. One of my favorite scriptures is Proverbs 18:16 KJV: "A man's gift maketh room for him, and bringeth him before great men." The main takeaway from this Scripture is that God has entrusted us with abilities that not everyone has. As we use these gifts to serve Him, He receives the glory because the great men of the earth will acknowledge our gifts, by which we glorify the Giver.

For some of us, our gifts are not as apparent as the gifts we see in others. Our gifts may be to aid in some larger work. We may not view these gifts as talents, but they are just as important. Others of us are endowed with talents that are strikingly apparent and may be readily used to the glory of God. When we understand what our talents are, our duty in this life, we must do our utmost to put these talents to use for the Lord.

Another potent scripture regarding the use of our talents is 1 Timothy 4:14–16 KJV, which states: "Neglect not the gift that is in thee, which was given thee by prophecy, with the laying on of the hands of the presbytery. Meditate upon these things; give thyself wholly to them; that thy profiting may appear to all. Take heed unto thyself, and unto the doctrine; continue in them: for in doing this thou shalt both save thyself, and them that hear thee." Though this Scripture pertains to the gift of preaching the gospel, it relates to us all. All gifts, one or an array of them, are given to us by God to know more of Him and to use in helping humanity. As we use these gifts for our Maker, they double, or multiply. This directly corresponds to the parable of the talents in Matthew 25:14–30 KJV, where even the smallest talent is increased with use.

Now, how can you identify your talent? The short answer is simply to pray! Entreat the Lord as to your duty and He will show it to you in no uncertain terms. With prayer, you will see areas in which you are skilled or gifted. Perhaps your talent is not completely developed, and there may be character work to be done before you can use it. Not all talents are ripe when we recognize them; some must be developed. If you have any question in regards to your talent, work on your "spiritual fruit" until the answer comes (see Galatians 5:22, 23 KJV). You will begin seeing the purpose God designed for you. My testimony is a prime example of this.

My Talent Testimony

I have written poems since I can remember. These poems were for my own comfort, admonition, and exhortation. I considered, and still consider, myself a student of poetry, and I plan to be a learner in this area until I die. As a student, I did not think I was ready to release a poetic work in book form, but the Lord impressed me otherwise.

My love of poetry started as a child, before I could even read or write. I loved all things that rhymed. Because I could not read, often my parents or siblings would read poetic children's Bible stories and Christian poetry to me that I would do my best to commit to memory. My usual tactic was to make a song out of the words. All these many years later, I still remember some of those childhood books.

I incorporated poetry into almost everything I did. In school, any project that gave me leeway to be creative would get a "Samara Original," which would be generously rewarded by the graders. The reception of my poetry at home and at school clued me in that this might be a natural talent, but I did not know exactly how to use or develop it. I enjoyed writing poetry but felt my work was far below the poetry I loved.

As I grew older, I grew to cherish religious poetry focused on spiritual encouragement, as well as narrative poetry, especially poems relating historical events. Nearly every attempt to write the poetry I loved seemed lacking to me. It was almost like I was not yet ready to write these poems. Rarely would I share these with anyone. When I did share them with my family, they were generally well received, but to me, something was still missing.

Because these poems did not meet my ideal standard, for many years I wrote poetry simply for fun. The subject matter varied. I wrote poetry for my life events and for those of my friends and family—mainly weddings and birthdays. I also wrote poetry as I pondered nature. These poems were rarely religious.

During my freshman year of college, my mom found one of my religious poems and sent it in to be published in a book with many other poems. It was accepted and published, and I am grateful to my mom for being instrumental in publishing my first poem. However, during this time, I enrolled in a college poetry class, which killed any hope that I would ever write the kind of poetry that anyone would take seriously. The class was painful to me and within the first month, I dropped it. To compound this feeling of failure, another one of my poems was rejected by a campus poetry magazine. I decided to let random students read a few of my cherished poems, and I received mixed feedback, of which the negative feedback held power in my mind.

Consequently, poetry became an insignificant talent to me, as I pursued my other life interests. I had other talents to be developed on which I focused more concretely and seriously. However, when I wanted a creative release from the stress of developing my other talents, I would still write poetry. If my poems helped no one else, they helped me, if only as a creative release.

For a time, I could write and complete only secular poems, but it was difficult to create and to finish the godly poetry of my earlier years. I felt this was indicative of my spiritual temperature. Though I held on to the faith I believed, in many ways I wandered far from the Lord. I knew I needed a spiritual experience and often prayed for one, but I did not know this would lead to the most difficult trials in my life. But that is when everything started to change.

Indeed, a spiritual change came as I encountered monumental trials in life, which led me to truly see my need to surrender to the Lord. These trials made me self-examine and study the Bible as I never had before. These trials made me realize that I was not the Christian I had always professed to be. Only then did I desire to just sit at the feet of Jesus and truly learn of Him.

For the first time in my life, I not only read the Bible, but while reading also sat and gazed into the heart of God through meditation. I beheld beauty in the Word of God in ways I never had before. Indeed, the Bible had taken on a new life. It was alive and calling me to learn anew what I thought I already knew.

As I read the Bible, I realized that the faith I thought I had was mere sinking sand. I saw that I was not firmly rooted in faith because faith can be acquired only by an experience in God's words. Though I was a believer, I had a tiny faith—maybe the size of the smallest mustard seed. But I praise the Lord that even the most dwarfed mustard seeds grow!

Through the great teacher of the Holy Spirit, I saw that God was growing me in ways I had never imagined. Each day, I was truly climbing Jacob's ladder. At every rung there was a new experience and an invitation to go higher and higher by study, meditation, and surrender. It was no longer *my will* but *God's will* in every area of my life.

My work, my time, and my money all now belonged to the Lord. As I began to give up those sins I loved, life became a bit harder, but I would see even more things that I needed to change. The loss of friends, the rejection of some family members, and the change in circumstances are all part of the cross we bear when choosing God, seeking His kingdom and righteousness. At times, it was all I could do to hold on to the Mighty hand of the Lord and not give up! I am living proof that the Lord upholds all who fall (see Psalm 145:14 KJV).

In learning to trust the Lord through my dark hours, I had finally understood that being a Christian is a daily experience and not something you just declare that you are. This was a true awakening, as I had grown up a Seventh-day Adventist, and not in a nominal household either. My parents taught the very same present truth to which I am drawn today. Truth never changes, but the light of truth grows (see Proverbs 4:18 KJV). I finally understood that being a "Christ follower" meant continually pressing toward the mark for the prize, come what may (see Philippians 3:14 KJV). It is a life of work and faith! It is daily sanctification because sanctification is an ongoing process from which we gain power and strength through communing with the Lord by reading His Word and by earnestly praying to Him for His help and power.

Sanctification is an active process. There is no such thing as a dormant Christian. All true Christians are active within their sphere of influence! If your sphere of influence is small, then work the sphere God gave you. One talent can gain usury as did the five talents (see Matthew 25:14–30 KJV). We are God's witnesses to actively work where He has put us (see Isaiah 43:10–12; Acts 1:8 KJV).

I am not surprised that during the worst trials of my life, my ability to write religious poetry became nearly effortless. My connection with the Lord was real. It was mature and intelligent. I saw His hand in every aspect of my life. During my darkest crisis,

I felt as Joseph must have on his way to Egypt. I learned a great deal in a little time.

During this time, meditation upon themes of my Christian walk would produce poetry that I felt must be shared. This was the first spark of my evangelistic spirit. I shared because I wondered if others were like me and needed to be awakened to the deeper truth and richer experience, especially if they were lifelong Christians with a dormant experience. I wondered if they really knew that active obedience, the right-doing part of faith, shows our love for God, not just our flowery words of lip service. People see our actions before they believe our words.

During this time, I added more people of like faith and those Christians who seemed to desire to obey God's Word to my social media account. I desired fellowship and to share the poems I was writing regarding our Christian experience. Adding more people produced more opportunity for negative feedback, but it did not affect me as it did when I was an undergraduate student. Criticism no longer mattered to me; only God's purpose for me mattered. Glorifying God mattered.

My zeal to study and learn Bible promises, prophecy, and procedures was proportionate with my desire to share more. It was only at this stage in life did my lifelong talent of poetry truly become relevant to me. This talent, like every talent God gives us, was one of my means to evangelize the world. Indeed, I aim to use it to the glory of God until I cannot use it anymore.

When I think of the journey that inspired this book of poems, I am in awe, and my heart rejoices because I know God is leading. He wanted me to hear His voice and not my own. He wanted me to awaken to righteousness and to be obedient before

He used me to His glory. I praise the Lord I did not harden my heart as the dark trials came upon me. I praise Him that I looked to Him for help and surrendered to His will. He rewarded me in ways above all I could ask or think! This is an ongoing process, and I still daily make the choice to serve the Lord.

Poetry is a talent I thought would never be used in the way the Lord is using it now. God's timing is always perfect, and His way is always right. I pray my testimony gives hope to someone who is struggling to use the talent, or various talents, given to serve the Lord. Your talent may need to be developed, but trust in the Lord to lead and guide you in its use. May the Lord ever bless you as you seek to serve Him!

Use Your Gifts!

The Lord gives each of us at least one talent to use. For you, it may not be poetry but something else. Time is something we all have that we can devote to the Lord. How we use our time is important to our spiritual growth and to the spiritual growth of others. Besides time, you may possess exceptional oratory, organizational, or people skills. Talents include health, time, influence, speech, kindness, and much more. These talents may be enveloped in a profession or simply may be gifts given to a person (see Ephesians 4:8, 11–13; 1 Corinthians 12:4, 8–10 KJV). In short, your talent can be anything with which God has blessed you to bless others; however, please know that your talent can be used wisely or unwisely.

I wanted this book to begin with a call to action because I have spoken to so many men and women who neglect to use even their most apparent talents. I too am guilty of making excuses for not using all of mine. The reasons for this neglect vary but may encompass:

- The talent is not fully developed.
- The person may have a lack of finances.
- The person may be extremely introverted.
- The person may lack personnel or a team.
- The person's location may not be conducive.
- The talent is not exclusive (i.e., others possess the same talent and seem more skilled in using it).

It is important to note that these are all debilitating excuses. When God gives you a gift, He gives you a way to use it.

We must seek the Lord in prayer for His way to use and develop our talent. Maybe you are prone to take the glory and not return it to God. Correcting this may take a maturity you do not now possess. There may be a bucket of reasons for God not making the way for you to use your gift, but you must seek Him with self-examination for the answer. When trying to find your gift, it is best to begin with developing the fruit of the Spirit (see Galatians 5:22, 23 KJV). By focusing on character development through prayer and self-examination, you will in verity be focusing on using your talent to the glory of God until the answer comes.

Now, I must warn you to never compare your gift with someone else's gift. God does not call us to compare any talent to that of another, but to use what we are given, even in the humblest sphere of influence. Use the gift you have as only you can!

Poems for God's Glory

The poems in this book range from the very simple to poems that will make you ponder the times in which we are living today before the soon coming of the Lord. I pray the paired scripture verses elevate your thoughts and lead you to examine the related reading for even more context and insight. I urge you to look up each scripture and be inspired to dig even deeper into these things.

I pray this poetical work inspires you to grow closer to Christ, yielding to Him your life and talents. He will indeed show you all things that pertain to life and godliness (see 2 Peter 1:3, 4 KJV). He will show you His will for your life and will work in you to do it (see Philippians 2:13 KJV). He does not give any talents to be hidden under a bushel, but all our talents must be rightly used to glorify Him. We are God's lights in the world. (See Matthew 5:14–16 KJV). If your desire is to glorify God in your body and in your spirit, you will be used in His service (see 1 Corinthians 6:20 KJV)! Lastly, I pray that as you read, you will be inspired to aggressively evangelize the world.

In addition to the poetry, this book has a section in which I briefly discuss how we may maintain our Christian walk. Many Christians ask: "How do we keep our energy up as we walk through life's pressing trials?" I pray this section will provide practical answers. There is also a brief discussion on end-time Bible prophecy to shed further light on some of the prophetic last-day events showcased within my poems. May the Lord bless and encourage you with hope and godly fear as you read this book. MARANATHA!

"

There is no one like you in the whole world! God has made you unique to use your talents/gifts for Him in a way that only you can. Begin using your talent for His glory today! Do not delay! Inaction is effectively making a choice against the Lord. Moses once asked Israel in a time of apostasy, "Who is on the Lord's side?" (Exodus 32:26 KJV). May your response to this question always be, "I am!" Show Him your loyalty by your active hands and brains. May God bless every effort you make on His behalf!

End-time Events

Poem 1

The Legal End of Protestantism

*And he exerciseth all the power of the first beast before him, and
causeth the earth and them which dwell therein to worship the first
beast, whose deadly wound was healed.*
REVELATION 13:12 KJV

The death knell rang in the air,
But many were not made aware
That evangelicals agreed to slant
All that was ever Protestant.

In 1517 it did rise
By Luther's theses contrariwise
To papal error and lavishness
'Gainst God's faith and righteousness.

In October on day thirty-one,
This new era had then begun.
But the papists called the protest strife,
Though it gave our conscience life,
And from it sprang a nation free
With principles of liberty,

Where people from all nations/lands
Dream to step upon its sands!

And the thing that makes this nation great
Is the separation of its church and state;
But the papal wound is only healed
Once this separation is repealed.
For only then can it revive
Its supremacy, which is its pride.

So, now the Mother Church has regained
Those daughters who would seek her fame.
These daughters have their Mother's look,
For so it's written in the Book
That her image will afterward bring about
A shaking of the remnant out
By a decree, a mark or seal,
That forces all against their will
To worship on a day not blessed
Instead of the seventh day of rest
(Child, adult, male, or female
May not either buy or sell
Without the mark in forehead or hand,
Enforcing worship by a man
In opposition to God's command).

It takes *patience* and *faith* to stand,
But after that . . . the Promised Land.

Exactly 500 years to the day,
Protestantism was *legally* signed away.
Just one step left, so hold on steady,
And be ye warned,
Get ready! Get ready! Get ready!

Poem 2

The Coming Crisis

And through his policy also he shall cause craft to prosper in his hand;
and he shall magnify himself in his heart, and by peace shall destroy
many: he shall also stand up against the Prince of princes; but he shall
be broken without hand.
DANIEL 8:25 KJV

A crisis on the earth does loom
As consequence of a healing wound
Of that union of both church and state:
To religious conscience legislate,
To force all to worship a day not blessed
Instead of God's seventh day of rest,
By force restricting temporal needs
Unless all adhere to her decrees,
To forsake the heavenly Father's plan
And obey the traditional law of man.
A first-day worship will make everyone
Bow to a man who upholds the sun.
He calls himself *Vicar of our Christ,*
While he denies Him by his very life.

You see, the U.S. Congress chose to bring
The pope to America to crown him king
Of peace to the nations united, and then
To all in league with this Man of Sin.
Though most readily adopt his *Laudato Si'*,
This book rejects our liberty.
For though Sunday worship is at its core,
It points to nature and earthly poor.
He moves in darkness but hit the lights!
You'll see the annihilation of our Bill of Rights.
Religious freedom—see, Protestants understood!—
Is valueless to the politics of the Common Good.
Yet evangelicals have joyfully and legally reached
Across to papists to mend what was breached.
In 2017 on the 31st of October,
They declared aloud Luther's protest was over.
After 500 years with point of a pen,
Rome's daughters returned to their Mother again.
Even now, atheists have joined in this movement
To rest the earth for climate improvement.
Even the trade unions are coming together
To save humanity from this inclement weather.
And financial strongholds are tumbling down
To create a new order most think will be sound.
Temporal prosperity will cause very many
To sell their soul for a digital penny.
All of these things will soon culminate
Into a fight 'gainst our Great Potentate.

All who warn others of this crisis might
Be killed, or imprisoned, e'en put into flight.

Father, I pray that each dissenter
Would not have to flee in cold or in winter,
Nor on the Sabbath day of the Lord,
That we may worship together in one accord.
Lord, I pray the state of that summer will be
Suitable for a weekday flight to safety.
And may we each shout with alarm the events of this story
As the remnant raised up, proclaiming Your glory.

POEM 3

The Lord's Soon to Appear

" "

And ye shall hear of wars and rumours of wars: see that ye be not troubled: for all these things must come to pass, but the end is not yet. For nation shall rise against nation, and kingdom against kingdom: and there shall be famines, and pestilences, and earthquakes, in divers places.
MATTHEW 24:6, 7 KJV

Shout it aloud with voice and with pen:
  "Jesus Christ is coming again!"

The signs are converging to mark the world's end.
Yes, it's for certain—He's coming again!

First a mere rumor and now there's a war.
Can you see it, or do you need more?

And a pestilence global is within the land;
This is also a sign that Christ is at hand.

And then there's calamities with great devastation.
People are protesting nation 'gainst nation.

A global food shortage is coming in on the rear,
As seeds, farms, and bees seem to just disappear.

A religious revival is soon to come in the land,
And the foolish will join it but the wise understand.

A law, apparently Christian and mild in its spirit
Will speak as a dragon, forcing all earth to fear it.

Also, laws to solve poverty are soon to arrive,
Creating an even wider financial divide.

There will be rich and there will be poor,
But those of the middle class will be no more.

These are the signs, which were long prophesied,
Indicating this earth has not long to abide.

The antichrist is to become the Man of Peace,
And many will bow to make these signs cease.

Six six six is the number of this man
Who causes craftiness to prosper in his hand.

All of his policies the world will obey;
They will give him their conscience at the end of the day.

And at this time, within this demand,
The remnant of God will all seal their stand.

These events will come in rapid succession.
Now is the time! *Awake!* Learn the lesson!
Now is the time! *Awake!* Make confession!
Now is the time! Put away all transgression!

Study the Bible prophecies meant for this time,
And run with the wise, not the foolish and blind.

This is about worship, and power's the plan.
I pray we obey God and disregard man.

Those in the Light will exercise free choice;
We'll rejoice in the Truth—and always rejoice!

Though the signs show the final crisis is near,
We would see Jesus, and He's soon to appear!

POEM 4

Even So, Jesus, Come!

" "

He which testifieth these things saith, Surely I come quickly. Amen.
Even so, come, Lord Jesus.
REVELATION 22:20 KJV

In the church, very many today
Are losing their faith and falling away—
And, so close to the close of earth's history—
As prophecy's revealing Iniquity's Mystery,
Whose healing is very nearly complete,
Once church and state in unison meet.

See, the laws of America—the land of the free—
Will soon counteract its lamb's liberty.
The whole world's being placed on a wagon.
America, the lamb, will speak as a dragon.
And America, in this final generation,
Will enact laws purposed for papal domination.
The pope's influence increases as the end nears
Over the seven sociocultural spheres.*

Government and media are working as one
To hurry us on to worship the sun.
Nature worship within a Global Climate Compact
Will take away our freedoms and not give 'em back.
And, just let me say this, so you are told—
The COVID crisis was based on a cold.
Twenty-twenty, in many ways prophetic,
Drilled us within the Hegelian dialectic:
Produce the crisis and give the solution,
Bringing the earth to rapid conclusion.
Masks were mandated all over the States
And lockdowns created at-home inmates—
Not just in body but also in mind—
As they watched the news, reason declined.
Propaganda's taken down many a voice
That's upholding the freedom of personal choice.
So, many gave their health up to science
After being urged to offer compliance
To whatever the untested remedy would be
For America to get to immunity,
Which incidentally was already created in man
To fight off the objects cells naturally ban.
Injecting a virus into your body
Is not a practice that's for the godly.
Scripture says that our body's a temple.
We maintain it with remedies, natural and simple.
This panacea was a world lab created
To make us a people amalgamated—

Like those animals in the days of Noah's flood,
Contaminated, not having clean blood.
The blood is the life of all creatures, you see.
We should keep it pure, contaminate-free.
Fear and fortune are disarming the thinking
And at broken cisterns many are drinking.
No one knows the damage already begun
In the name of science unethically done.

All seeing these events know time is short.
Now we must prepare and others wisely exhort.
For we are now within a great testing time,
As the events of the world become really sublime.
We must stand in our lot as the children of God,
Though labeled "straitlaced," "extremists," and "odd."
We must strive to keep Christ within our center
By blocking the avenues Satan can enter.
The Scripture promises we must strive to remember,
In order each day all to Jesus surrender.
Every principle of our faith will be tested sore,
For this is a physical and spiritual war.
Hold high God's Eight Natural Laws of Health!
Study and practice them, for they are our wealth!
All other labor will soon from us cease.
Destruction is coming as men pronounce peace.
An evangelistic spirit is aggressively needed
To plant the gospel in hearts—globally seeded.

Soon, we'll see a harvest from the work that we've done,

And we'll collectively pray, "Even so, Jesus, come!"

---

*Seven Mountains of Societal Culture:

1. Business 2. Government 3. Media 4. Arts and Entertainment 5. Education
6. Family 7. Religion

POEM 5

In Our Trying Hour

" "

Because thou hast kept the word of my patience, I also will keep thee
from the hour of temptation, which shall come upon all the world, to try
them that dwell upon the earth.
REVELATION 3:10 KJV

"Bless me, Lord, or I will not let go"
Is a great prayer for this time of woe.
Every Christian will face persecution;
Faith in the Lord is our only solution.
Wrestling with God, from what I can tell,
Is the experience we all need to prevail.

Prophecy's fulfilling on every side.
There's no place to just run and hide,
Except under the Almighty's wings,
To ease the sting of our sufferings.
We now have entered the Small Time of Sorrow.
Let's work for today, as not promised tomorrow!
Now is the time—our day of salvation!
Let's pray always and watch the revelation
Of prophecy fulfilling in each daily event,
And prepare ourselves: forsake sin and repent

Of all of the wrongs that we have done
To God and our brethren. Be united as one!
Plant the promises of God deep in our heart.
Once hidden in there, they cannot depart.
But they ensure that our faith remains strong
And looks up to Jesus as we press along,
Each trial testing our faith moment by moment
As we live within this Day of Atonement.
Let's surrender our sins to our Intercessor:
Our great High Priest, Jesus, forever.
We must have faith that always sees clearly
Up to God's Way in His sanctuary,
That surrenders our will, come what may,
And holds firm to principle to endure all the way.
One simple prayer shows we have won:
It's "Lord, not *my* will but *Thy* will be done!"
Then Christ Himself will give us the power
To do His will in our trying hour.

P O E M 6

The Coming Test

" "

Beloved, think it not strange concerning the fiery trial which is to try
you, as though some strange thing happened unto you: But rejoice,
inasmuch as ye are partakers of Christ's sufferings; that, when his
glory shall be revealed, ye may be glad also with exceeding joy.
1 PETER 4:12, 13 KJV

A test will come to every soul,
To prove us metal or refined gold.
This test is concerning the Law of God,
Whether to honor His Sabbath or it to downtrod.
This test requires study and a lot of it,
Because we must understand the counterfeit
Is a day set up by papal authority
For its world domination and superiority.
The first day, Sunday, will be highly upheld;
All will bow, be exiled, or suffer in jail.
See, no individual conscience will be allowed to reign
To further true revival and uphold God's name.
Every dissenter may die a martyr's death
If they cling too rigidly to the truth they profess.

The New World Order is the Old World rule
Of the Common Good policy—dissent is treated cruel.
But a tiny Remnant will, aloud and bold,
Speak prophetic words the Bible foretold.
Their words will enlighten and shake the globe,
And in great tribulation they'll have the patience of Job.
Many by their blood will a testimony spread,
A witness when alive and a witness when dead.
I pray God keep His people as His charge they lead,
For they will not bow! Their blood will be *seed!*

POEM 7

Redemption's Nigh

> "
>
> *And when these things begin to come to pass, then look up, and lift up your heads; for your redemption draweth nigh.*
> LUKE 21:28 KJV

I only seek to make it clear:
The Coming of Christ is almost here.
All of the signs that was said to be
Are happening now in synergy.

We are entering now the Small Time of Trouble,
And all of our efforts we'll have to redouble.

The war on terror and the war on health
Are wars and rumors of war in stealth.
Then, there's nation rising against other nations,
Which is synonymous to our race relations.
And famine is coming—an abundance of lack—
Based upon drought, war, or cyberattack.
And global pestilences have changed our lives,
With forceful mandates prophesied to arise.
Policies to get the world inoculated
Coincide with efforts to depopulate it.

And climate policies result in depression,
As weather events occur in succession.
Earthquakes, floods, and severe storm predictions
Further policies with liberty restrictions.
And all who understand prophecy will sound the Loud Cry
As they look up rejoicing that redemption is nigh!

POEM 8

The Prophetic Pendulum

Turn not to the right hand nor to the left: remove thy foot from evil.
PROVERBS 4:27 KJV

Earth's last events are aligning with force.
Its pendulum's swinging with might.
The greater the push and swing to the left,
The more rapid the swing to the right.

Faith

POEM 9

Faith Comes by Hearing God's Word

So then faith cometh by hearing, and hearing by the word of God.
ROMANS 10:17 KJV

"Faith is not feeling," so it is said—
Though both are a belief in kind.
One believes God's promises;
The other's a state of mind.

Faith is the unseen evidence
While hoping in God's Word.
When praying back these promises,
We can know that we are heard.

God has told us time and again
His words are as good as done.
So, as we pray believing them,
We know that victory's won.

Let us study on to be approved,
Clad with the armor's sword,
To be fortified against the time when we're
Persecuted and abhorred.

For our faith must stand firm amidst
The want of pure religion;
In this trying time, all that we'll have
Is a "God said it" or "It is written!"

POEM 10

Tomorrow's Faith Today

Take therefore no thought for the morrow.
MATTHEW 6:34 KJV

The faith we need tomorrow
Is the faith we'll gain today
From the trials within each hour,
That leads us to obey
God's Word in times of testing.
His promises are sure,
For those who believe His every word,
On them His blessings pour—
First like the dew of summer
And then like the autumn rain.
It's faith that gives the sustenance
So that blessings may remain.
Faith only comes by hearing
And applying the Word of Life,
Which is comforting and pleasant
But can cut just like a knife.
Be mindful not to shun it
When it hits you to the core.

As faith is never feeling,
Let's obey, though wounded sore.
We need a faith enough to weather
Hunger, weariness, and delay,
And as we believe in all God's promises,
He'll give us power to obey.

P O E M 1 1

A Mustard Seed Faith

If ye have faith as a grain of mustard seed, ye shall say unto this
mountain, Remove hence to yonder place; and it shall remove; and
nothing shall be impossible unto you.
MATTHEW 17:20 KJV

Faith as a grain of mustard seed
Is really not that small;
A plant springs from this tiny seed
Into the greatest herb of all.

If you think it's a tiny faith,
You take the saying wrong,
For "faith as a grain of mustard seed"
Implies your faith grows strong.

A tiny faith can never move
The mountains in our way.
We ask the Lord, "Increase our faith!"
To yield from day to day.

And a lofty tree grows from this seed
With branches for the fowls,
So may our faith branch out to hold
Up others in their trials.

Faith is never feeling;
It's the hope in and of the Light.
We must possess it 'til the end,
To have victory in this fight.

Faith is a gift of the Spirit fruit
And works additions in our lives;
As we do and hear the Word of God,
It reforms us and revives.

So, yes, faith must spring as from a seed
And grow ever in ascent.
Jesus saying "O ye of little faith"
Was not a compliment.

We must have great faith!
And, as the *promise* is in the seed,
The heart planting of the Word of God
Gives us the faith we need.

POEM 12

Unexpected Faith

❝

And he said unto Jesus, Lord, remember me when thou comest into thy kingdom. And Jesus said unto him, Verily I say unto thee, Today shalt thou be with me in paradise.
LUKE 23:42, 43 KJV

Now when the centurion, and they that were with him, watching Jesus, saw the earthquake, and those things that were done, they feared greatly, saying, Truly this was the Son of God.
MATTHEW 27:54 KJV

Imagine a faith that sees Jesus as King
While sharing in His crucified suffering!
The dying thief knew the Messiah had come
When he said, "Lord, remember me when Thou comest into Thy kingdom."
He saw victory where another saw loss
In the wounded body next to his cross.
He could've chosen on that Sabbath's eve
Not to see a Saviour in whom to believe.
Oh, but how great was the faith of that dying thief!
May we all meditate upon his story of belief!

Again, imagine a faith that sees Jesus as Christ
While upon the cross, giving His life!
The centurion saw evidences of divinity
Shining through dark events 'round Calvary.
"Truly, this was the Son of God," this soldier said,
Right after the Messiah died, hanging His head.
This centurion's faith quite simply stood out
By believing the moment when many would doubt.
Imagine his faith growing strong as he hears it
Uttered, "Father, into Thy hands I commend My spirit!"

POEM 13

For Our Good

" "

And we know that all things work together for good to them that love
God, to them who are the called according to his purpose.
ROMANS 8:28 KJV

Let it ever be understood
That God is working for our good.
Whatever trials may come about,
He's sure to work the whole thing out.

So, we need neither to worry nor to pout
But hold to His *promises* without one doubt.

For as we pray His Holy Word,
We have certainty that we are heard.
So, though we see nothing from day to day,
We may safely trust in His will and way.

POEM 14

Uphold Me, Lord!

``

The LORD upholdeth all that fall, and raiseth up all
those that be bowed down.

PSALM 145:14 KJV

Lord, You uphold all those who fall,
And I take You at this promise.
I choose to simply walk by faith,
Not as a Doubting Thomas.
My heart evokes one constant plea:
"Help me keep my strength in Thee!"

Prayer

POEM 15

Sweet Smelling Savor

And lead us not into temptation, but deliver us from evil: For thine is
the kingdom, and the power, and the glory, for ever. Amen.
MATTHEW 6:13 KJV

Our Father, who art in Heaven,
Thank You for this time we're given
Before Your Kingdom comes again
To banish the sting of death and sin.
May in all the earth Thy will be done,
Just as it is above the sun.
Thank You for Christ's work above,
Interceding for us through Your Love:
For His grace and pardon before the Throne
To give us Your acceptance as His own.
We ask for gifts of holy need;
For the Spirit's fruit we humbly plead,
For with this fruit may You us bless
And cleanse our hearts as we confess
Our besetting sins for which we wrest,
As we press forth unto righteousness.
May we gain all victory over sin
By believing Your words through faith within.

And as we forgive quickly everyone,
Forgive us likewise through Your Son.
Give us each day our temporal needs,
So we may serve others with kindly deeds.
May we let self on the day's cross die,
By beholding Christ Jesus, Your Son, on high,
By looking up through His Word of Life,
And by pleading His promises to ease our strife.
May the fiery trials that give us pause
Thoroughly fit us for Your applause
In Thy Kingdom of power and glory forever,
When all of the saints shall be gathered together.
Help us with Thy power every evil overcome.
This I humbly pray in the name of Your Son.
Oh, Most High God, may this prayer quickly ascend
To You with the sweet-smelling savor of Jesus; Amen!

POEM 16

More of Thee!

" "

He must increase, but I must decrease.
JOHN 3:30 KJV

"Less of me and more of Thee!"
Indeed, this is my constant plea,
As I go about my day
In this world of self-display.

Give me, Lord, of Thine own privilege
To form me wholly in Thine image,
Because I keep Thy testimonies
Within the Word, which Thou hast shown me,
That point from me and to Thee only.

"Less of me and more of Thee!"
Give me spiritual eyes to see
Selfish snares Satan's sure to set
To trap me deeply within his net.

"Less of me and more of Thee!"
From all my sins, please set me free.

Anoint my eyes to read Thy story.
Help me manifest Thy glory!

"Less of me and more of these!"
Lord, I am down on bended knees,
Praying prayers for others too.
Please, help them also be like You!

POEM 17

These Trials, Praise the Lord!

> ❝
>
> *Knowing this, that the trying of your faith worketh patience. But let patience have her perfect work, that ye may be perfect and entire, wanting nothing.*
> JAMES 1:3, 4 KJV

Every day I go to Jesus;
In the morning when I rise.
I know not what event will happen—
It may come as a surprise.

I have learned to keep a constant
Stream of prayer ever raising high,
For in the moment I'm not watching,
The cruel tempter does draw nigh.

And these moments are so crucial
'Cause all the good it seems I've done
Comes in question should I falter,
And it'll seem the tempter's won.

But I know that Christ is victor;
He will put the foe to flight.
And in place of my weakness give me
Lots of strength to bear the fight.

For each trial is for my patience,
And I shall choose to bear each well,
For He gives me faith to conquer,
And for His grace, there's no parallel.

Praise the Lord for *prayer*, I tell you!
Praise the Lord for *patience* too!
Praise the Lord for my *endurance*,
And those **songs* to get me through!

---

* "Song is a weapon that we can always use against discouragement"
(*The Ministry of Healing,* p. 254.8).

POEM 18

Seek the Lord in Prayer

"

Create in me a clean heart, O God; and renew a right spirit within me.
Cast me not away from thy presence; and take not thy holy spirit from
me. Restore unto me the joy of thy salvation; and uphold me with thy
free spirit.
PSALM 51:10–12 KJV

Apart from the sights and sounds I hear,
Three times a day and anywhere,
I bring my praise, troubles, and all care
To the Most High in prayer.

Hid in my closet, I daily share
My deepest needs, though He's well aware.
'Til I have strength, I stay in there,
Pouring out my soul in prayer.

I specify with intense pleas
My great desires upon my knees.
Only He's strong enough to bear,
So, I surrender all in prayer.

"Give me a clean heart," I do say,
"And my old spirit, please take away.
Thy Holy Spirit take not, I pray.
Make salvation sweet today."

Within this *psalm it's very clear:
Asking in faith keeps His presence near.
And "Lord, search my heart (drive away each snare),"
I speak His words in prayer.

And, while upon my knees I be,
My prayer becomes intercessory.
I pray that we all white garments wear.
So, I plead His grace in prayer.

Ask God for food or to end despair
'Cause He sends us blessings everywhere.
Deficient devotion is a dangerous dare,
So, may we seek the Lord in prayer!

---

* See also Psalm 139:23, 24 KJV.

POEM 19

Pray First!

. . . your heavenly Father give[s] the Holy Spirit to them that ask . . .
LUKE 11:13 KJV

I'm about to tell you something
Of which you may be unaware:
When you read the Word of God,
You must first begin with prayer.

Prayer is the very key,
Unlocking stores of divine treasure.
So, just ask, for it will be given you—
God's Spirit without measure.

Prayer is the breath of the soul.
It's the secret of spiritual power.
It's how we keep the Lord in view
Each day, hour after hour.

So, as you study day by day,
Please take time to stop and pray.
For truth, the very best way to prepare
Is making sure the Spirit's there.

POEM 20

A Simple Prayer

> " "
>
> *Because thou sayest, I am rich, and increased with goods, and*
> *have need of nothing; and knowest not that thou art wretched, and*
> *miserable, and poor, and blind, and naked: I counsel thee to buy of me*
> *gold tried in the fire, that thou mayest be rich; and white raiment, that*
> *thou mayest be clothed, and that the shame of thy nakedness do not*
> *appear; and anoint thine eyes with eyesalve, that thou mayest see.*
> REVELATION 3:17, 18 KJV

Lord, my pride and my arrogance
Wholly subdue;
Help me ever to see my need
Of a Saviour in You!

POEM 21

Thankful Praise

In every thing give thanks: for this is the will of God in
Christ Jesus concerning you.
1 THESSALONIANS 5:18 KJV

Prayer and praise go hand in hand,
So, give God thanks as much as you can!
It will never hurt to let God know
You appreciate all that He does bestow.

God gives us above what we ask or think,
As our prayer with His joyous praise we link.
See, as we appreciate His loving power,
We may raise our Ebenezers every hour.

POEM 22

Prayer and Praise

> **"**
>
> *And at midnight Paul and Silas prayed, and sang praises unto God:*
> *and the prisoners heard them.*
> ACTS 16:25 KJV

In winds of war, in times of strife,
Let's thank the Lord for sparing life.

For this we know He does us spare
To exalt His name and with others share
Our testimony of His great care.
So that in distressing times they'll be aware,
Though times be tough and days uncertain,
There's a remedy to soothe their hurting.

Our Great Physician gives us hope
By showing us His Way to cope,
Which is to lift our eyes in stormy days,
Exalting Him with prayer and praise!

POEM 23

Strong Prayer Life (Daniel)

" "

Now when Daniel knew that the writing was signed, he went into his house; and his windows being open in his chamber toward Jerusalem, he kneeled upon his knees three times a day, and prayed, and gave thanks before his God, as he did aforetime.

DANIEL 6:10 KJV

Serving God takes real courage—
To stand alone come what scare.
Standing firm to principles
Takes a lot of fervent prayer.

God's Word cites many examples
For the trials we'll go through;
Daniel is just one book with much
Encouragement to you!

In his youth with his three fellows,
Daniel's diet was the test—
Asking for water and for pulse
Instead of wine and flesh.

Daniel knew our daily diet
May create a temperance bind,
So, he chose to only eat the food
That would build his strength and mind.

The diet God gave in Eden—
They knew it was the best,
And, after eating it for three whole years,
They scored high above the rest.

Far surpassing other men
In all knowledge, skill, and wisdom,
God gave Daniel understanding
Pertaining to a dream or vision.

God's gift to Daniel saved them all,
The king had ordered dead.
It prophesied the world's kingdoms—
Right from Babylon, the head.

Later in Daniel's lifetime,
Another plot was stayed.
Deceitful men tried to end his life
On account to whom he prayed.

Daniel survived the den of lions,
And those lions others slew—
And just how God back then saved Daniel,
He's now saving me and you.

O, to have the strength of Daniel,
Holding strong to what is right!
We may all have the strength of Daniel
Because the Lord God was his might!

POEM 24

God Supplies

But my God shall supply all your need according to his riches
in glory by Christ Jesus.
PHILIPPIANS 4:19 KJV

God supplies my every need
When to His will and way I heed.
I simply come to Him and ask,
But He seldom answers very fast.

His delay causes me to examine
My heart and soul for godly famine.
Then, if I fail to see my sins,
I read His Word for greater lens.

In there, His Spirit helps me see
Why this want was not for me,
Or after delaying a year or more,
Heaven's windows shower o'er.

Praise the Lord for His will and way,
To supply my needs from day to day!
See, even when His blessings linger,
In *patience* I may trace His finger.

Bible Reading and Study

POEM 25

Study Time

> ❝
>
> *These were more noble than those in Thessalonica, in that they received the word with all readiness of mind, and searched the scriptures daily, whether those things were so.*
> ACTS 17:11 KJV

Tick-tock, tick-tock, resounds the clock
As we read the written scroll.
Yes, study often the Word of God,
And see it line upon line unfold.

Daniel and the Revelation
Are the books to study now,
That reveal what's coming at the end,
As we seek to be heavenbound.

The Bible interprets itself.
Do not depend on men!
It's packed with the unlocking keys
From Inspiration's pen.

So, study on to know the Lord
And His revelations of what is near.
May your efforts ever grow your faith,
To believe the truths you hear!

POEM 26

Godly Wisdom

"

Behold, thou desirest truth in the inward parts: and in the hidden part
thou shalt make me to know wisdom.
PSALM 51:6 KJV

The wisdom that we want the most
Is given by the Holy Ghost.
Delving deeply into God's Word,
Our hearts and souls are rightly stirred.

There, we are moved to better know
The way of truth in which to go.
Understanding comes from every verse
That we in thought and in deed rehearse.

See, something known just has no might
Without prompt actions for the right.
Doing right is righteousness,
And wisdom comes from nothing less.

The Word of God is our sure guide
To eternal life at Jesus' side.
So, may we ever through all our strife
Make it plain that we *choose life!*

POEM 27

Lighted Pathway

> "
>
> *Thy word is a lamp unto my feet, and a light unto my path.*
> PSALM 119:105 KJV

My free will gives to me consent
Of how my days in life are spent.
I will to find a private nook
To contemplate God's sacred Book.

See, tempting trials of every day
May quickly rush into my way,
If I do not focus in my mind
On things which can alone refine.

The Bible gives to us complete
A path for our ever wand'ring feet.
It shows us all the golden way
Of how we ought to spend our day.

So, no matter where in life I go,
I repeat the sacred words I know,
So that my feet do not dare depart
From God's lighted pathway in my heart.

''

Each day we must spend dedicated time, even a thoughtful hour, with God in order to grow in confidence, love, and power to do His will. One way to do this is to make it a habit to commit at least one scripture to memory each day for daily comprehension. Read the scripture at least ten times aloud, along with its citation, slowly and clearly. Then, challenge yourself to recall the verse from memory using only the citation. Do not move on to another Bible verse until you have this one stored deep within your memory and you clearly understand its meaning. As you recite it, meditate upon it with prayer, asking God to reveal the meaning by His Holy Spirit. Actively live out this verse in your life. This is how we store the Word of God in our hearts and minds, grow closer to Him, and grow in favor with God and man.

POEM 28

Daily Devotions

❝❝

Evening, and morning, and at noon, will I pray, and cry aloud: and he
shall hear my voice.
PSALM 55:17 KJV

I drink in God's presence.
Our time is a jewel—
More precious than gold.
It uplifts my soul.

Nourished by worship,
My prayers flow like incense.
His Words are my manna,
So sweet in my mouth.

I savor God's Law.
It's sweeter than nectar,
More enduring than time.
It stays on my mind.

Lord, the world and its attractions
Sour when You're near.
To steadfastly behold You
Gives me great cheer!

Morning and evening,
I hunger for You,
Ever praying at noontime
To be stronger in You!

"

Did you know that we are to regularly meet with God—at least three times a day? Psalm 55:17 KJV states that "Evening, and morning, and at noon, will I pray, and cry aloud: and he shall hear my voice." So, put this into practice! Make time in the morning for prayer and personal devotion. At noon, stop what you are doing and worship God in prayer and meditation. At evening, with prayer and thanksgiving, praise God for His mercies throughout your day. Make these seasons of worship special and delight yourself in the Lord!

Pillars of Faith

POEM 29

What is the Sabbath?

❝

Wherefore the children of Israel shall keep the sabbath, to observe the sabbath throughout their generations, for a perpetual covenant. It is a sign between me and the children of Israel for ever: for in six days the LORD made heaven and earth, and on the seventh day he rested, and was refreshed.

EXODUS 31:16, 17 KJV

The Sabbath's a sign;
The Sabbath's a seal.
It'll make the difference
Before whom we kneel.

It came before
There was even a Jew;
So, it's for all
Who would be true.

Of God's Holy Ten,
It's Number Four,
Revealing God's name,
Land, title, and more.

When Christ returns,
This day, Number Seven,
Will even be worshipped
By all those in heaven.

For a sanctified Sabbath,
Which God hallowed and blessed,
Was created for man
And given for rest.

So, when we worship
To God we should say,
"Thank you, Creator,
For the Sabbath Day!"

POEM 30

Second Advent: End-time Messages

"

Let us hear the conclusion of the whole matter: Fear God, and keep his commandments: for this is the whole duty of man. For God shall bring every work into judgment, with every secret thing, whether it be good, or whether it be evil.

ECCLESIASTES 12:13, 14 KJV

There are Three Angels' Messages,
But they all agree in one,
Though they're distinct entities,
Like God: Father, Spirit, Son.

The first angel sounds a warning
That Judgment Day is here,
That the gospel must go to every land
So that Christ can soon appear.

The second warns of Babylon
And its scarlet-colored wine.
It calls all people out of her
Who have a godly mind.

The third angel warns of worship—
A false day against a true,
As those who keep all God's commands
Will not bow to Billy Blue.

The Mark is Sunday worship
Enforced globally in the land.
Your forehead has your choices;
Your actions are with your hand.

I pray we heed the gospel,
Though this means we'll be at war.
For Satan's wrath will persecute
Those loving Jesus more.

May patience and faith preserve us!
May the crisis be ever swift!
May we sound the Three Angels' Messages,
Prepared for harvest sift!

P O E M 3 1

The State of the Dead

" "

The dead praise not the LORD, neither any that go down into silence.
PSALM 115:17 KJV

"When you die, you go to heaven."
This is mainly what is said
To bring comfort to most everyone
In relation to the dead.

But biblically speaking,
The dead are in the ground,
Not alive and praising God,
As they cannot make a sound.

They're not watching over you
From their dusty grave.
There's no life or breath within them
To care how you behave.

There's no love nor hatred anymore.
All their envy's gone,
And a body without a living breath
Cannot be living on.

Our breath is our body's spirit.
It's how God gave us life.
God breathed into dust this power,
And when we die, it goes back to Christ.

If faithful, He'll resurrect us
To live in the sweet by and by,
But if we already go to heaven,
This resurrection is a lie!

For the Bible says so plainly
The dead in Christ shall rise.
At the last trump we shall be changed
And meet Him in the skies.

POEM 32

The Sanctuary

And let them make me a sanctuary; that I may dwell among them.
EXODUS 25:8 KJV

The earth once had a sanctuary
Patterned off the true,
Where a lamb in type was offered up
In the place of me and you.

The priest would daily sprinkle blood
Before the inner veil,
Symbolizing Christ's covenant of blood,
Which allows us to prevail.

On the day of the atonement
And in great humiliation,
All must put away their sins
And to God alone confess them.

One unblemished ram or goat
Was for the congregation slain.
His blood sprinkled upon the mercy seat
Seven times for a cleansing to begin.

The sin was also placed upon
A goat fated to escape,
As Satan will bear all sins
The righteous did forsake.

A fit man would then take this goat
And lead him from the fold,
Representing Satan's lot
In the millennium foretold.

Type has now met antitype
Since eighteen forty-four.*
Christ is now in the Most Holy Place
Until this cleanse is o'er.

Now is the time to be at one
With our High Priest in heaven.
In deep humility of soul,
Let's make sincere confession!

For He's coming back again
When His sanctuary's cleansed
For all those who have spotless robes
Once this controversy ends.

---

* On October 22, 1844, Christ entered into the Most Holy Place in the heavenly sanctuary to begin the work of investigative judgment, according to the prophecy of Daniel 8:14 KJV.

POEM 33

Justified, Sanctified, Glorified

> **"**
>
> *And such were some of you: but ye are washed, but ye are sanctified, but ye are justified in the name of the Lord Jesus, and by the Spirit of our God.*
>
> 1 CORINTHIANS 6:11 KJV

Justification's an imputed work
Granted by Christ the moment
We plead, "Forgive me, Lord,"
As He *immediately* bestows it.

Sanctification is a *progressive* work—
A right decision every moment.
But we're only fully sanctified
Through Christ's pardoning atonement.

Yes, sanctification is a daily work.
We'll do it all life-long,
Surrendering those things to God
That we know we're doing wrong.

Daily upon our cross we'll die
Praying, "Lord, help me to do Your will!"
He'll give us all we need each day
To conquer by this appeal.

Then, glorification we'll await
When Christ comes in the sky.
We'll be clothed with immortality
In the blinking of an eye!

POEM 34

The Spirit of Prophecy

❝

Despise not prophesyings.
Prove all things; hold fast that which is good.
1 THESSALONIANS 5:20, 21 KJV

A prophet is among us.
Her name is Ellen White,
Inspired by the Holy Ghost
Who told her what to write.

A prophet is among us
For these ending times—
A help in reading the Word of God
As a light unto the blind.

A prophet is among us,
Though physically she's dead.
But her words live on to reveal events
Predicted way ahead.

A prophet is among us,
And you only have to read
To see how these inspired words
Shed radiant light indeed!

POEM 35

Eight Laws of Health

"

Beloved, I wish above all things that thou mayest prosper and be in health, even as thy soul prospereth.

3 JOHN 2 KJV

Eight natural laws exist for man
For abundant health in his lifespan.

They're meant to restore human creation
Into God's image through reformation.

These eight laws expand and expand
To make up all of *God' s Plan* for man.

Find these health laws written in caps
Throughout this poem to keep you on track.

TRUST IN GOD daily,
Awake early for prayer.
Then, go EXERCISE
In the fresh morning AIR.

Soak in that SUNSHINE
Throughout your day.
Drink plenty of WATER—
In ounces, half what you weigh!

Eat a plant-based PROPER DIET,
Having no more than three meals
Spaced five to six hours apart—
For having more than that kills.

Abstain from what's bad;
Always TEMPERANCE keep.
Last one: Go to bed early—
By 9 p.m. be asleep.

See, REST is beneficial
For both the body and the soul,
Like resting the seventh day,
Creation's Sabbath of old.

These Eight Laws of Health
In connection with God's Ten
Make up the *physical* and *moral* laws
God gave to save from sin.

POEM 36

The Baptism

> **"**
>
> *Therefore we are buried with him by baptism into death: that like as*
> *Christ was raised up from the dead by the glory of the Father, even so*
> *we also should walk in newness of life.*
>
> ROMANS 6:4 KJV

I drowned in Christ's arms, but I didn't die.
To drown there meant to live.
With great delight there,
I spent my life there,
Buried in the Life that He chose to give.

Daily Christian Life

P O E M 3 7

Victory in Jesus

" "

Blessed is the man that endureth temptation: for when he is tried, he
shall receive the crown of life, which the Lord hath promised to them
that love him.
JAMES 1:12 KJV

The loveliest man I've ever known
Sits by His Father on the right of His throne,
Pleading His blood on account of my sin,
Saying, "Dear child, I have caused you to win!"

"But you must want it, and there' s work to do.
Repent and forsake sin; become born anew.
Ask for My merits and plead them each day−
For whosoever comes to Me, I will not cast away.

"I stand at the door of your heart and knock.
You may open and fall on Me, your Savior and Rock:
For to break on Me will cause you to mend,
For I'm more than a Savior; I AM also your friend.

"Know that My love will bring out your best.
In trials you'll be weary, but in Me you'll find rest.

In this fire of affliction, your dross will melt away;
And you'll shine like pure gold at the end of the day.

"True heart conversion will garner the crown,
And your fruit of the Spirit will be seen all around.
Your sweet experiences will be bitter one day,
But cast not off your faith—be watchful and pray!"

POEM 38

Contented Praise

Not that I speak in respect of want: for I have learned, in whatsoever
state I am, therewith to be content.
PHILIPPIANS 4:11 KJV

"Here today, gone tomorrow"
Can be said of joy or sorrow.
Within one second of a day,
All that's dear may go away.
Within one minute of an hour,
Every gloom may lose its power.
In a life that's full of change,
We have a Savior within our range.
He tells us always, "Be content,"
And in sharing sadness reticent,
Unless a help our story brings
To someone else's sufferings.
He tells us also, "Flee from sin,"
And a merry heart He'll put within.
So, may thankfulness fill all our days
As we example a life of praise!

POEM 39

Deeds of Kindness

And be ye kind one to another, tenderhearted, forgiving one another,
even as God for Christ's sake hath forgiven you.
EPHESIANS 4:32 KJV

Deeds of kindness on our pathways
Beam radiant warmth as loving rays.

For fragrant acts like flow'rs perfuming
Sweeten life, keep friendships blooming.

Our deeds of love are by others cherished,
Especially when their hope is perished.

POEM 40

No Outward Beauty

> "

> *For he shall grow up before him as a tender plant, and as a root out of a dry ground: he hath no form nor comeliness; and when we shall see him, there is no beauty that we should desire him.*
>
> ISAIAH 53:2 KJV

He had no outward beauty
That men should Him desire,
Yet in the hearts of all sincere,
He lit a flame of fire.
His love and His compassion
And His unique humility
Invited all to follow
When He said, "Follow Me."
Not by words alone
He taught them;
His disciples learned the most
By the life He lived—
He caught them
To fish beside all coasts.

POEM 41

Choice

> "
>
> *I call heaven and earth to record this day against you, that I have set*
> *before you life and death, blessing and cursing: therefore choose life,*
> *that both thou and thy seed may live.*
> DEUTERONOMY 30:19 KJV

A thin line
Spreads across the slate,
And this line borders
Both *love* and *hate*.

On this line,
A clash abides,
And abstracts here
Stay side by side.

This slender line
Is like a gate
That swings into
Both *love* and *hate*.

For this line swings
To our inner voice,
As it's nothing more
Than human choice.

POEM 42

Let God Avenge!

> "
>
> *Dearly beloved, avenge not yourselves, but rather give place unto wrath: for it is written, Vengeance is mine; I will repay, saith the Lord. Therefore if thine enemy hunger, feed him; if he thirst, give him drink: for in so doing thou shalt heap coals of fire on his head. Be not overcome of evil, but overcome evil with good.*
>
> ROMANS 12:19-21 KJV

Revenge is a sickness—
It has to be!
Each day it destroys
Our harmony.

Revenge comes with hatred
And ruins quite deep.
O, help, dear Father,
Your erring sheep!

Revenge is for God!
He'll do it right.
Please take heart—
He'll win our fight.

For God can revenge
Any His neighbor.
But if we interfere,
We'll gain His disfavor.

POEM 43

The Lord's Battle (David)

> ❝
>
> *. . . for the battle is the LORD's . . .*
> 1 SAMUEL 17:47 KJV

A giant threatened Israel.
Goliath was his name.
For forty days he challenged them
And laughed when no one came.

But God told David take the stand,
Although he was so small,
And He would give him all the might
To make this giant fall.

David had a little sling,
But he trusted in God's power
To bring Israel deliverance
In their anxious hour.

One stone of five
Caused a forward dive
Of the giant like tumbling lead,
And once on the ground,
Goliath's sword was found
Cutting off his head.

Both camps were shocked
At the twisted plot.
The Philistines then fled
From Israel's joy
Because a little boy
Had done as God had said.

May this story ever come to mind
Whenever we're in a fight—
For God redeems us surely when
We trust *only* in His might.

Marriage and Courtship

POEM 44

End-time Marriage Counsel

> "
>
> *And as it was in the days of Noe, so shall it be also in the days of the Son of man. They did eat, they drank, they married wives, they were given in marriage, until the day that Noe entered into the ark, and the flood came, and destroyed them all.*
>
> LUKE 17:26, 27 KJV

One of the signs for these last days
Is that marrying will be a craze.

Marriage as given by the Lord
Unites male and female in one accord.

Symbolically, it shows the love of Christ,
Giving His life to save His wife.

Far from this ideal, please trust
That most marriages are based on lust.

Because courtship seems to never run its course,
Many marriages end up in divorce.

But the time of divorcement would never be,
If couples sought God's remedy.

He'd tell them that self-surrender
Is paramount to stay together.

He'd say the "Us" that's cherished
Can only thrive when the "Me" is perished.

God called the wife a very good thing,
Never sanctioning the pagan ring
But because her character's second to none.
Her godly ideal is Proverbs 31.

The husband is to abide in God's favor,
Known of all for his godly behavior.
To lead his household he must strive.
His godly ideal is Ephesians 5.

Their uniting focus is not chemistry
But would they benefit God in ministry.

In their search to find true love,
Each heart first linked to God above.

And united in God's unfailing cord,
Their labors will have good reward.

The answers to their prayers are done
Because they two agree as one.

POEM 45

Considering Marriage?

" "

Can two walk together, except they be agreed?
AMOS 3:3 KJV

Do not marry just for pleasure,
But seek to gain eternal treasure.

Let marriage be just the thing
That fits you for the coming King.

Pray and question before you leap,
For wedded bliss and peaceful sleep!

Consider — Are we tidy? Can he till?
Can she cook a healthy meal?

Is he lazy or well-read?
Can she make a loaf of bread?

Is he manly? Is she calm?
Would we ever cry to mom?

Is he frugal? Can she save?
Will his appetite behave?

Is she jealous? Is he strong?
Can she stay at home for long?

Is he selfish? Is she kind?
Will we keep the Lord in mind? —

And, many more questions ask in prayer,
For God will surely make you aware
Of traits regarding your future spouse
That will ruin your union or divide your house.

Shun uniting upon a feeling;
Unite your souls to reach God's sealing.

In this sealing, husband and wife,
Have in view eternal life.

See, if heaven is our "Ever After,"
Consider it the premiere factor.

Seek godly counsel and please be wise!
Seek the mate that God supplies
(And even then shun courtship lust)!
Pray always! Keep God your trust!

POEM 46

Overcoming Lust

Having therefore these promises, dearly beloved, let us cleanse ourselves from all filthiness of the flesh and spirit, perfecting holiness in the fear of God.
2 CORINTHIANS 7:1 KJV

Hot today and lukewarm tomorrow
Will lead you to eternal sorrow.

The exhortation spoken to one today
May be for the speaker down the way.

Only steady movements of the soul
Can keep us from going down that road
Of perdition when having lust of heart,
That makes our love of truth depart.

One thing will help us win the fight
Is guarding well our appetite.

For "man shall not live by bread alone"
But by every word from off God's throne.

The power is in God's holy promises
To conquer our own Doubting Thomases.

Do your best to memorize,
"I have made a covenant with my eyes,"

And "sin shall not have dominion over you."
These promises are tested, tried, and true—

And lots more promises there are to prize
That will make a lustful fool be wise.

Let's deny self from every lust
And yield our will to godly trust.

It's our only advantage to overcome,
For Jesus is the only One
Who can defeat Satan in His might,
But our will must be given to do right.

See, abiding in Christ is how we win.
It is how to gain victory over sin.

Meditations

POEM 47

Affirmations of the Unseen

"

For the invisible things of him from the creation of the world are clearly seen, being understood by the things that are made, even his eternal power and Godhead; so that they are without excuse.
ROMANS 1:20 KJV

Crimson gray
Describes today—
No gleam, bright clouds, or blue.
Out on the bay
Some people lay
Without Sun rays, not seeing You.

Pale cold waves
Without Sun glaze,
No golden sparkling hue.
Yet with amaze
I shouted praise,
"You're Abba! You're God! You're True!"

The darkest days
And harshest phase
Cannot reject Your power.
Your grace abounds,
You're all around
To direct us at each hour.

The invisible
We've come to know
By Your physical reveal.
The sand, the sea,
The marine anemone—
All testify that You are real!

And, since there can be
What we don't see,
Like a God of abundant love,
Teach us each day
To follow Your Way
In the Most Holy Place above.

P O E M 48

Jesus Always Watches

"

The eyes of the LORD are upon the righteous, and his ears are
open unto their cry.
PSALM 34:15 KJV

The eyes of the LORD are in every place, beholding the
evil and the good.
PROVERBS 15:3 KJV

O, what a tender thought sublime
That Jesus watches all the time!
We're never ever all alone
Without our Spiritual Rock or Stone.

Though Satan may tempt us for the wrong,
Be sure to know that God's real strong.
And just as He counts your teeny hairs,
He sees all things and *always* cares.

POEM 49

Love Weathers All

A friend loveth at all times, and a brother is born for adversity.
PROVERBS 17:17 KJV

O that love were like an evergreen!
O that flowers never faded!
O for the constant stream of love
In friendships thought betray'ed.

Pure love is like an evergreen,
Strong and long abiding.
In friendship, it weathers every tempest
If God is there and guiding.

POEM 50

Christian Love

> **" "**
>
> *He that loveth not knoweth not God; for God is love.*
>
> 1 JOHN 4:8 KJV

What does love mean
To those whose hearts are unclean,
To those whose eyes are not sore
By the mass of the poor,
To those whose feet do not go
Where there's heartache or woe,
To those whose hands do not feel
The defeat of the ill,
To those whose mouths do not speak
To those up the creek?

Their love is weak.

God's love is strong,
Lasting lifelong.
And I know His love feels
Our feverish ills.
I know His heart breaks
When Christians are fakes

And when their haughty pride
Hurts the less fortunate side.
We should all take note
Of the infamous quote:
"Unto them do
As your desire to you."

God's love is true!

POEM 51

Where Credit Is Due

“ “

. . . for without me ye can do nothing.
JOHN 15:5 KJV

I've got to give credit
Where credit is due.
And all the credit, dear Lord,
Goes always to You!

The Call

POEM 52

Cry Aloud, Spare Not

" "

Cry aloud, spare not, lift up thy voice like a trumpet, and shew my people their transgression, and the house of Jacob their sins.
ISAIAH 58:1 KJV

If my cry were soft to spare,
Would those in need be made aware
Of the sins within the house of God
And of the evil paths they trod?
To me, the Bible makes it clear,
"Cry aloud" and do not spare,
And like a trumpet lift your voice
To bring the people to a choice:
To serve God or to serve man,
To cease abominations in the land.
These transgressions are so clear.
Revive, awake, *awake* to hear
God pleading to depart from sin
With reformations for the end!
Some will vaguely speak the truth,
Which tends to deaden its reproof,
While some will be afraid to act,
And in this conflict, they'll cite tact:

Saying, "There's no love; you're overzealous!"
So—let the people stay rebellious?!
I pray to God that's not their reason
To not be instant out of season,
And pray that all come off the fence
And uphold God's love with obedience.
I pray the Lord His servants stand
Not on the wisdom of a man
But on the all-wise Word of God
Though labeled singular and odd.
May God keep us as they prod
And may God reap us while they prod.

POEM 53

Let's Get Them Wide Awake!

"

And that, knowing the time, that now it is high time to awake out of
sleep: for now is our salvation nearer than when we believed.
ROMANS 13:11 KJV

A clock is counting down to doom,
But are all wide awake?
A preparation must begin right now,
For soon the earth will quake! . . .
And after that a lake
In which the wicked bake!
There's quite a lot at stake!
Let's get them wide awake!

POEM 54

Sweet Peace

"

There is no peace, saith my God, to the wicked.
ISAIAH 57:21 KJV

No matter how you try
To wash sorrows by,
Do you end up in a pail of tears?
Your vying, your trying
Without help from God's Son
Seems useless—only long, wasted years?

The bird up in the sky,
O, look how he flies!
And just think, God's guiding him.
So, without delaying, start praying.
With God by your side,
You'll be free, having His peace within.

POEM 55

Fallen Away?

❝❞

For the Son of man is come to save that which was lost.
MATTHEW 18:11 KJV

Tell me, dear youth . . .

Have you fallen away, fallen away?
Have you decided to "do you" before the dawn of the Day?

Are the "frogs, snails, and puppy dog tails"
    Or the "sugar, spice, and everything nice"
Worth the loss of your eternal life?

Are the chains and rings of the floss and bling
Worth turning your back on Christ the King?

Is the fun or hype or the booze or pipe
Worth putting down the Christian fight?

Are gender rights or a political stand
Worth revolting 'gainst the Son of Man?

Is a hug, a kiss, or a fleeting pleasure
Worth giving up a lasting treasure?

Is a sporting game or a gaming trend
Worth losing salvation in the end?

Are houses, cars, or even a job
Worth wandering away from God?

Is the music, makeup, or a fashionable look
Worth your name not being in God's Book?

Is one day of walking down an aisle
Worth losing your Redeemer's smile?

Is the desire upon your fork and knife
Worth not feasting at the Tree of Life?

Are worldly wisdom/philosophies
Worth rejecting God's abundant pleas?

Is your hope to be just like the rest
Worth not keeping the Sabbath* blessed?

Is entertainment's dazzling awe
Worth the forsaking of God's Law?

Is finding the truth too hard to carry
Worth not being in God's sanctuary?

To some of these, I once affirmed,
But I praise the Lord that I've returned.

Yes, I took a road away from home,
But in God's mercy I no more roam.

See, no surety was in my path,
For in the distance, I saw great wrath.

And, I did not want God's wrath for me,
So, I bowed to His grace and tender mercy.

The text on which my heart laid hold
Was: "What can a man give in exchange for his soul?"

Then, a promise I've grown deeply to cherish
Is: God bears long, "unwilling that *any* should perish."

Now I intercede in prayer for youth
That your eyes obtain the Light of Truth.

I pray you all will count the cost
Of choosing not to bear your cross,

And that the victory over self is won
Before earth reaches its setting sun.

---

* The seventh-day Sabbath: Genesis 2:1–3; Exodus 20:8–11 KJV.

P O E M 5 6

Stretched Out Still

"

For all this his anger is not turned away, but his hand is
stretched out still.
ISAIAH 9:12, 17, 21 KJV

When is there going to be a better way?
The very hearts of men are growing chill.
"For all this his anger is not turned away,
But His hand is stretched out still."

More than objects to which we bow and pray,
We give our idols time; time from God we steal.
"For all this his anger is not turned away,
But His hand is stretched out still."

There's vanity in what we do and say;
We use the name of God as no big deal.
"For all this his anger is not turned away,
But His hand is stretched out still."

We forget that Sabbath's on the seventh day,
Which God set apart and gave His seal.
"For all this his anger is not turned away,
But His hand is stretched out still."

Parents have children who simply don't obey.
They say, "It is Corban," and "Bend to our will!"
"For all this his anger is not turned away,
But His hand is stretched out still."

Binding ourselves into bundles of hay,
Many lie and cheat and steal and kill.
"For all this his anger is not turned away,
But His hand is stretched out still."

For materialistic things we pay,
Wanting what's not ours is a selfish thrill.
"For all this his anger is not turned away,
But His hand is stretched out still."

We must do God's will while it is day.
Please! . . . Fall on the Rock, 'cause Christ is real.
He's coming soon with judgment; so, please do not delay.
Surrender all! God loves you . . . still!

P O E M 5 7

Peace

“ “

For he is our peace, who hath made both one, and hath
broken down the middle wall of partition between us.
EPHESIANS 2:14 KJV

The wars, the wars, the wars will not cease,
But right in the midst, God gives us sweet peace.

To worldwide famine, there is no release,
But God feeds His people, giving them peace.

Pestilence is causing population decrease,
But God is our healer, and so we have peace.

Severe weather events are on the increase,
But God is our shelter and gives us His peace.

No matter the event or the alarm,
God's people are safe always from harm.

The promise is that we'll dwell in safety
Under the arms of God Almighty!

Book and Bible References

BOOK AND BIBLE REFERENCES

Related Reading

" "

Study to show thyself approved.

2 TIMOTHY 2:15 KJV

- POEM 1: The Legal End of Protestantism
  - ○ *Revelation 13:12*; 13; 17:1–6; Amos 9:9; Luke 22:31; Ezekiel 16:44; Genesis 2:1–3; Exodus 20:8–11; 14:12–16 KJV
- POEM 2: The Coming Crisis
  - ○ Revelation 13; Genesis 2:1–3; Exodus 20:8–11; Acts 5:29; Daniel 7:25; *Daniel 8:25*; 2 Thessalonians 2:3–12; Revelation 17:3–6, 13, 15, 18; Daniel 11:43; James 5:1–5; Revelation 14:6–12; Matthew 24:20; Revelation 18:1–4 KJV
- POEM 3: The Lord's Soon to Appear
  - ○ John 14:3; Revelation 1:7; *Matthew 24:6, 7*, 1–8, 14, 20, 24; Luke 21:11; **Testimonies for the Church, Volume 5, p. 452.1**; Revelation 13:3, 12–18; Daniel 12:10 (see also Matthew 25:1–13); James 5:1–6; Daniel 8:25; 1 John 2:22; John 8:44; Psalm 94:16, 17; Revelation 6:17; Testimonies for the Church, Volume 9, p. 11.2; **Selected Messages, Book 2, p. 391.5**; 2 Timothy 2:15; Acts 17:11; Revelation 12:17; 7:3, 4; 14:1–5; 2 Corinthians 6:2; 1 John 1:9; Daniel 8:14; 9:24–27; Exodus 34:5–8; Revelation 13:15, 17; 14:9, 10; 2 Thessalonians 2:3, 4, 11; Matthew 4:9, 10; Isaiah 14:14; Acts 5:29; John 1:1–4; John 14:6; Philippians 4:4; John 12:20, 21; Revelation 22:11, 12, 20 KJV.

- POEM 4: Even So, Jesus, Come!
    - o 2 Thessalonians 2:1–3, 7–9; Revelation 13:11–17; 17:9; Matthew 24:6–8; Genesis 6–8; 9:4; Leviticus 17:11; Daniel 12:14; James 4:7–9; 2 Corinthians 10:4, 5; John 9:4, 37, 38; 3 John 2; Exodus 15:26; Mark 16:15; 2 Corinthians 9:6; Galatians 6:9; *Revelation 22:20* KJV.

- POEM 5: In Our Trying Hour
    - o *Revelation 3:10*; Job 23:10; Genesis 32:26; 24–28; 2 Timothy 3:12; Psalm 91:1–4; Matthew 24:6–8; Mark 1:14, 15; Acts 3:19; John 5:16; 2 Peter 1:4; Matthew 16:19; Hebrews 11:6; Luke 21:28; Daniel 8:14; Hebrews 7:25; 9:11; 4:14–16; Psalm 77:13; John 14:6; Matthew 26:39; Luke 22:42; Joel 2:23; Hosea 6:3; Matthew 13:24–30; Revelation 4:10, 11; Acts 1:8; Galatians 5:22, 23 KJV.

- POEM 6: The Coming Test
    - o Job 23:10; Genesis 2:1–3; Exodus 20:3–17; 2 Timothy 2:15; Revelation 13; 14:9, 10; 18:1; James 5:7–11; Isaiah 43:12; Acts 1:8; Matthew 24:14; Revelation 14:12, 13; 6:10; Revelation 17:6; 2:10 KJV; **The Great Controversy, p. 41.3**.

- POEM 7: Redemption's Nigh
    - o Matthew 24:6–8; Mark 13:4, 7, 8; Luke 21:9–11; Revelation 13:15–17; Matthew 25:6; *Luke 21:28* KJV.

- POEM 8: The Prophetic Pendulum
    - o *Proverbs 4:27*; Matthew 24:1–8; Luke 21:9–11; Revelation 13:3; 11–17; James 5:1–6; Daniel 8:25; Revelation 14:9, 10 KJV.

- POEM 9: Faith Comes by Hearing God's Word
    - o Mark 11:24; 2 Peter 1:4; Psalm 27:13; Hebrews 11:1; Isaiah 55:11; Jeremiah 1:9, 12; *Romans 10:17*; Hebrews 4:12; 1 Thessalonians 2:13; 2 Timothy 3:12; James 1:27; Matthew 4:4, 7, 10; 2 Timothy 2:15 KJV.

- POEM 10: Tomorrow's Faith Today
    - o *Matthew 6:33, 34*; 2 Peter 1:4; Matthew 4:4; Deuteronomy 32:2; Philippians 4:19; Romans 10:17; Hebrews 4:12; Philippians 2:13; 4:13 KJV.

- POEM 11: A Mustard Seed Faith
    - o **The Desire of Ages, p. 431.3**; *Matthew 17:20*; Luke 17:5; Matthew 13:31, 32; Luke 13:19; Ephesians 2:8; Revelation 14:12; Hebrews 11:1; John 1:9; Galatians 5:22, 23; 2 Peter 1:5–7; Romans 10:17;

Testimonies for the Church, Volume 1, p. 620.1; Galatians 2:16; Romans 12:3; Matthew 6:30; Matthew 8:26; Matthew 8:5–13; Acts 13:23; Romans 9:6–9; Galatians 3:16; Matthew 13:23 KJV.

- POEM 12: Unexpected Faith
  - o *Luke 23:39-43*; Daniel 9:25–27; Luke 23:42, 52, 54; *Matthew 27:54*; Mark 15:39; Luke 23:46 KJV.
- POEM 13: For Our Good
  - o *Romans 8:28*; James 1:6–8; John 13:7; Matthew 6:9, 10; **Selected Messages, Book 3, p. 172.3**; John 14:6; Psalm 77:13; Isaiah 55:8, 9, 11; Romans 11:33 KJV.
- POEM 14: Uphold Me, Lord!
  - o *Psalm 145:14*; 2 Peter 1:4; 2 Corinthians 5:7; John 20:24–29; Mark 9:23, 24; Philippians 2:13; 4:13 KJV.
- POEM 15: Sweet Smelling Savor
  - o *Matthew 6:9-13*; Hebrews 4:16; 7:25; Galatians 5:22, 23; Psalm 51:10–12; 1 John 1:9; Hebrews 12:1–4; Acts 4:12; 1 Corinthians 15:31; Ephesians 4:32; John 1:29; 12:32; 1:1–3, 14; 14:6; 1 Peter 4:12, 13; Job 23:10; 2 Corinthians 2:15; Ephesians 5:2 KJV.
- POEM 16: More of Thee!
  - o *John 3:30*; 2 Corinthians 3:18; Psalm 51:10–12; Psalm 139:23, 24; Psalm 119:2; 1 Thessalonians 5:23; John 5:39; 1 Peter 5:8; Luke 4:18; Romans 6:22; John 8:31–36; John 9:11; Revelation 3:18 KJV.
- POEM 17: These Trials, Praise the Lord!
  - o Romans 5:1–6, 1 Corinthians 15:57; 2 Corinthians 12:9–11; Hebrews 4:16; 1 Thessalonians 5:17; *James 1:2–4*; James 4:7; Revelation 2:10; 14:12; Romans 5:3–5 KJV.
- POEM 18: Seek the Lord in Prayer
  - o *Psalm 51:10-12*; 91:1; 139:23, 24; Hebrews 4:16; Revelation 6:11; Isaiah 55:6–9; Ephesians 6:10–18 KJV.
- POEM 19: Pray First!
  - o Luke 11:13; Acts 4:31; 8:15; John 14:16; 16:13 KJV.
- POEM 20: A Simple Prayer
  - o *Revelation 3:17, 18*, 14–21; Luke 18:10–14; Ephesians 2:8, 9 KJV

- POEM 21: Thankful Praise
  - *1 Thessalonians 5:18;* Philippians 4:4; Psalm 100; Hebrews 13:15; Ephesians 3:20; 1 Samuel 7:12 KJV.
- POEM 22: Prayer and Praise
  - *Acts 16:25*; Psalm 46:10; 2 Corinthians 3:2; John 16:33; Jeremiah 8:22; Psalm 42:11; John 14:6; Luke 21:28 KJV.
- POEM 23: Strong Prayer Life (Daniel)
  - *Daniel 1, 2; 6; 6:10*; Genesis 1:29; Zephaniah 3:17 KJV.
- POEM 24: God Supplies
  - *Philippians 4:19*; Matthew 7:7, 8; Luke 11:13; 2 Timothy 2:15; John 16:13; Malachi 3:10; 2 Corinthians 4:16; Psalm 8:3, 4; 1 Peter 5:6; John 10:29; Psalm 23 KJV.
- POEM 25: Study Time
  - *Acts 17:11*; 2 Timothy 2:15; 2 Timothy 3:16, 17; Isaiah 2:19; 13:13; 28:9, 10, 13; Romans 10:17; Revelation 1:3 KJV.
- POEM 26: Godly Wisdom
  - *Psalm 51:6*; John 16:13; Hebrews 4:12; John 14:6; Romans 10:17; James 2:14–26; Isaiah 11:2, 3; Proverbs 23:23; Proverbs 4:5, 7; 1 John 3:7; Psalm 119:172; Exodus 20:3–17; 1 Corinthians 1:30; Psalm 119:105; Deuteronomy 30:19 KJV.
- POEM 27: Lighted Pathway
  - Genesis 4:7; Deuteronomy 30:19; *Psalm 1:2*; *119:105*; Matthew 6:33; 1 Corinthians 10:5, 13; Deuteronomy 11:17–19; Joshua 1:8 KJV.
- POEM 28: Daily Devotions
  - Matthew 5:6; Psalm 51:11; John 4:14; Psalm 141:2; Revelation 8:3, 4; Matthew 4:4; John 6:58; Psalm 19:10, 7; Psalm 34:8; Psalm 1:2; Matthew 4:8–10; 2 Corinthians 3:18; *Psalm 55:17* KJV.
- POEM 29: What is the Sabbath?
  - *Exodus 31:16, 17*; Ezekiel 20:12, 20; Genesis 2:1–3; Exodus 20:8–11; Isaiah 66:23; Mark 2:27, 28 KJV.
- POEM 30: Second Advent: End-time Messages
  - Revelation 14:6–11; *Ecclesiastes 12:13, 14*; 1 John 5:7; Matthew 28:19; John 1:1–3; Matthew 24:14; Revelation 13:12–17; Exodus 20:3–17; 1 Thessalonians 4:11; Jeremiah 3:2–6; Revelation 12:12, 17; Revelation 14:12–16 KJV.

- POEM 31: The State of the Dead
  - *Psalm 115:17*; 6:5; Psalm 115:17; Ecclesiastes 9:5, 6, 10; Job 14:14, 20, 21; Acts 2:29, 34; Genesis 2:7; 1 Thessalonians 4:14–16; 1 Corinthians 15:52; Revelation 14:13 KJV.
- POEM 32: The Sanctuary
  - *Exodus 25:8-9, 40*; Leviticus 1:1–9; Leviticus 16:8, 14; 20–22; Hebrews 8:1–5; Hebrews 4:14–16; Leviticus 4:1, 2; John 14:6; Leviticus 23:27–31; Daniel 8:14; Psalm 77:13 KJV.
- POEM 33: Justified, Sanctified, Glorified!
  - *1 Corinthians 6:11*; 15:31; James 4:7–10; Philippians 2:13; 4:19; 1 John 1:9; Revelation 1:7; 1 Thessalonians 4:17; 1 Corinthians 15:52 KJV.
- POEM 34: The Spirit of Prophecy
  - *1 Thessalonians 5:20, 21*; 2 Chronicles 20:20; 2 Timothy 3:16, 17; John 16:13; 2 Peter 1:20, 21; 1 Corinthians 2:13; Isaiah 8:20; Revelation 14:13; Revelation 19:10; Isaiah 42:9; John 14:29 KJV.
- POEM 35: Eight Laws of Health
  - *3 John 2*; Exodus 15:26; Genesis 1:29; 3:18; Daniel 1:8–12, 15–17; Luke 13:33; 1 Timothy 4:8; Isaiah 55:1; Malachi 4:2; Ecclesiastes 11:7; 1 Corinthians 9:25; Genesis 2:7; Psalm 127:2; Matthew 11:28–30; Proverbs 3:5–8; Psalm 55:17 KJV.
- POEM 36: The Baptism
  - *Romans 6:4*; John 3:3, 5–8; John 1:4–9 KJV.
- POEM 37: Victory in Jesus
  - Hebrews 10:12; Acts 2:38: John 6:37; Revelation 3:20; Luke 20:18; Luke 4:18; John 15:14; Matthew 11:28–30; 1 Peter 1:7; *James 1:12*; Galatians 5:22, 23; Luke 22:42; Matthew 26:41 KJV.
- POEM 38: Contented Praise
  - Deuteronomy 31:8; *Philippians 4:11*; Matthew 6:15; 1 Timothy 6:6–8; Romans 12:15; 2 Timothy 2:22; Proverbs 17:22; Psalm 100:4 KJV.
- POEM 39: Deeds of Kindness
  - *Ephesians 4:32*; Matthew 5:16; Hebrews 12:12; 1 John 4:7, 8; 1 Corinthians 9:19–22 KJV.
- POEM 40: No Outward Beauty
  - *Isaiah 53:2*; Luke 24:32; Matthew 4:18–22; 1 Peter 2:21 KJV.

- POEM 41: Choice
    - Genesis 4:7; *Deuteronomy 30:19*; Joshua 24:15 KJV.
- POEM 42: Let God Avenge
    - Deuteronomy 32:35; *Romans 12:19–21*; Luke 18:3; Matthew 5:44; 2 Chronicles 20:15; Psalm 59 KJV.
- POEM 43: The Lord's Battle (David)
    - *1 Samuel 17:47*; 16:13, 18; 17; Psalm 136:24; Isaiah 26:4; Zephaniah 3:17; 1 Corinthians 10:11, 12 KJV.
- POEM 44: End-time Marriage Counsel
    - *Luke 17:26, 27*; Matthew 24:38, 39; Genesis 2:18; Mark 10:9; 1 John 3:16; 1 John 2:16; Philippians 2:3; 1 Corinthians 7:1–16; Exodus 33:5 (Isaiah 3:16–18, 21); Proverbs 31:10–31; Acts 6:3; 1 Timothy 3:2–5, 7; Ephesians 5:17–33: Joshua 24:15; Ecclesiastes 4:9, 12; Matthew 18:19 KJV.
- POEM 45: Considering Marriage?
    - *Amos 3:3*; Psalm 133:1; Genesis 2:20–25; Proverbs 5:18, 19; 1 Corinthians 7:27, 28, 33–35; 38–40; Hebrews 13:4; Philippians 4:6; Proverbs 11:14; 2 Timothy 2:22; Luke 18:1; 1 Thessalonians 5:17; 1 John 4:18; Proverbs 16:20 KJV.
- POEM 46: Overcoming Lust
    - *2 Corinthians 7:1*; Revelation 3:15, 16; 1 Corinthians 9:27; Job 31:1; Romans 6:14; (see also Genesis 39:9); Matthew 5:27–29; Luke 9:23; Luke 22:42; Romans 8:12, 13; 1 Corinthians 6:18, 19; 2 Corinthians 10:4, 5; Colossians 3:2, 5; 1 Thessalonians 4:3; 2 Timothy 2:22; James 1:12; 1 Peter 4:1, 2; 1 Peter 5:8, 9; 1 John 3:2, 3 KJV.
- POEM 47: Affirmations of the Unseen
    - *Romans 1:20*; John 3:16; Malachi 4:2; Mark 14:36; John 20:29; Romans 8:15; Galatians 4:6; 2 Corinthians 5:7; Colossians 1:15–17; 1 Corinthians 13:13; 1 John 4:8; John 14:6; Psalm 77:13; Hebrews 8:2; 9–10:22 KJV.
- POEM 48: Jesus Always Watches
    - Psalm 33:18, 19; *Psalm 34:15; Proverbs 15:3*; 1 Samuel 2:2; Psalm 18:2; 1 Corinthians 10:4, 13; 1 Peter 5:8; 2 Peter 2:9; Matthew 10:30, 31; Luke 12:7; 1 Peter 5:7 KJV.
- POEM 49: Love Weathers All
    - *Proverbs 17:9, 17*; 18:24; Psalm 133:1; 1 John 4:7 KJV.

- POEM 50: Christian Love
  - o *1 John 4:7-8*; Isaiah 58:5–11; 1 John 4:7, 8; Isaiah 53:3; Proverbs 16:18, 19; Hebrews 4:15; Matthew 7:12; 6; 1 John 3:10 KJV.
- POEM 51: Where Credit Is Due
  - o *John 15:5*; 1 Corinthians 10:17, 31; Philippians 2:13; Psalm 126:3 KJV.
- POEM 52: Cry Aloud, Spare Not
  - o *Isaiah 58:1*; Leviticus 18; 2 Timothy 4:2; 2 Corinthians 2:9; Romans 6:16; 1 Peter 3:16; Galatians 6:9 KJV.
- POEM 53: Let's Get Them Wide Awake!
  - o *Romans 13:11*; 2 Peter 3:3–15; Revelation 6:13–16; 20:12–14, 9, 10, 15; John 3:16 KJV.
- POEM 54: Sweet Peace!
  - o *Isaiah 57:20, 21*; Matthew 11:28–30; 1 John 1:9; John 15:5; Ephesians 2:14–18 KJV.
- POEM 55: Fallen Away?
  - o Mark 8:36; 2 Peter 3:9; Matthew 19:16, 17; 1 Timothy 6:12–16; *Matthew 18:11*; Matthew 6:19–21; Isaiah 43:1; 48:17; Revelation 22:1, 2, 27; Proverbs 6:23; Romans 2:13; Revelation 14:9, 10; 15:1, 2; 16:1; Lamentations 3:21–26, 32, 33; Ephesians 2:3–8; Hebrews 4:16; Luke 9:23; Colossians 3:3 KJV.
- POEM 56: Stretched Out Still
  - o Matthew 24:12; Exodus 20:3–6; Ecclesiastes 1:2, 14; Exodus 20:7; Genesis 2:1–3; Exodus 20:8–11; **Maranatha, p. 212.2**; Exodus 20:12; Mark 7:10–13 ; Matthew 24:40–42; **Selected Messages, Book 2, p. 143.3**; Exodus 20:13–16; Exodus 20:17; John 9:4; Luke 20:18; 1 Corinthians 10:4; Mark 1:15; Jude 1:15; 2 Peter 3:7, 9–13; Ezekiel 18:23; *Isaiah 9:12, 17, 21* KJV.
- POEM 57: Peace!
  - *Ephesians 2:14*; Matthew 24:6, 7; Isaiah 27:5; Luke 21:22–26; John 14:27; Luke 21:28; Psalm 91 KJV.

NOTE: All of the books in **bold** can be found through this book's **Suggested Resources** page using the link for Ellen G. White Writings. Scriptures listed in *bolded italics* are those given at the beginning of each poem.

Discussions

KEEP YOUR ENERGY!
Christian P.E.P.

> **"**
>
> *Wherefore seeing we also are compassed about with so great a cloud of witnesses, let us lay aside every weight, and the sin which doth so easily beset us, and let us run with patience the race that is set before us, looking unto Jesus the author and finisher of our faith . . .*
>
> Hebrews 12:1, 2 KJV

P ep is generally an energetic word. Many of us who attended secular schools may remember a pep rally right before a big season game. This was to infuse energy and excitement into school spirit for the support of the team. We who are Christians are rallying for something totally different than that of any secular sport emulation, which is part of the works of unrighteousness (see Galatians 5:19–21 KJV). But we still can benefit from godly pep infused into our Christian walk.

According to the Online Dictionary, pep, as a noun, means "energy and high spirits; liveliness." As a verb, the term means to "add liveliness or vigor to someone or something." The opposite meaning of pep is to "subdue," which means "to defeat, to overcome, or to crush." Therefore, the Christian walk would benefit from a daily jolt of pep to press toward the mark for the prize of the high calling of God in Christ Jesus, and not be overcome by the wiles of Satan.

Practically, how can this pep be applied in our daily life? Well, I have greatly benefited from a ministry that has put the practical applications of scripture as a tenet of their ministry. The ministry is called **Saved to Serve/Prophesy Again Ministries** (www.prophesyagain.org), which is under the leadership of a pastor who I first heard apply pep as an acronym, a simple and unforgettable acronym for our daily Christian experience.

Our Christian walk is fraught with divers and manifold hardships. We are at times defeated and crushed by trials that we never foresee. We do not know how to overcome these trials and tribulations; or we think we do know how to overcome them and find out that our wisdom only made matters worse. In our trials, we may look to Jesus, who has overcome the world (see John 16:33 KJV). He will know what to do for us. He gave us sure promises in His Word that we may use to overcome anything. We have precious promises, which are exceedingly great (see 2 Peter 1:4 KJV). We sometimes just don't know how to use these powerful promises to not be overcome by the foe. This is where pep applied practically helps uphold us when we feel down and undergo difficult experiences that challenge our Christian walk.

In the following paragraphs I relate this spiritual pep, practically applied, giving biblical examples from the Old Testament, to increase your hold upon the Lord and give you power to overcome. I also summarize each tenet with scripture promises that we all may claim to gain victories. Indeed, there are precious promises to increase our godly pep all throughout this section!

Practical Christian P.E.P.

We may practically infuse energy into our Christian experience with P.E.P., which stands for **P**atience, **E**ndurance, and **P**rayer! The acronym was fittingly derived from a passage in *Early Writings*, a book by Ellen Gould White, which relates the bitter cup that God has given His people to drink in order to purify and cleanse them. She states that "this bitter cup can be sweetened by **P**atience, **E**ndurance, and **P**rayer," and those who receive it will

"Put P.E.P. in your step with a song!"

have its designed effect upon their hearts and will honor and glorify God (p. 47). These three characteristic day-to-day activities are the critical energy of the Christian's life, but these can be infused even more energetically with song. A salient passage from *The Ministry of Healing*, also a book by Ellen Gould White, on p. 254.8 states, "Song is a weapon that we can always use against discouragement." We already know that the weapons that we can use to pull down the mightiest stronghold in our daily spiritual battles are not carnal (see 2 Corinthians 10:4 KJV). Consequently, any discouragement we feel can be beaten down and obliterated with singing. To this end, the Saved to Serve saying relates, "Put P.E.P. in your step with a song!"

Now that we have the acronym practically defined, I will relate each in more detail below so that we may better understand just how patience, endurance, and prayer are needed daily. If you truly read these poems, many of them relate how to practically fulfill this P.E.P. in our lives, but let's flush them out in prose. We'll begin with patience.

Patience

Let's talk about patience! According to the Online Dictionary, patience is "the capacity to accept or tolerate delay, trouble, or suffering without getting angry or upset." Patience is about attitude. A few synonyms to accompany the definition are: endurance, fortitude, restraint, tolerance, kindness, calmness, and staying power. Examining these synonyms reveal that the term patience is tied to our characters and the way in which we process our emotions. Patience in its purest sense shuns all the negative emotions tied to any trials we encounter.

I did not always know this. My basic definition of patience was just the ability to wait. We can wait and be entirely out of sorts and impatient about it. Consequently, the positive emotions expressed during a waiting period are indeed more conducive to possessing patience. Waiting on God means more than just having the ability to wait. It is having a calm assurance and a tolerant demeanor toward the negative situations in our lives.

Biblical examples of patience. Now, let's go to the Bible and find some examples from the Old Testament of those who were said to have patience. When we think of patience, we naturally think of Job. Job was known for his great patience in the midst of the most trying of conflicts (see James 5:11 KJV). He lost everything but still had a calm faith and acceptance of God's all-wise providence. Job 1:21 KJV reveals the purity of his patience toward God in the conflicts which quickly befell him: "The LORD gave, and the LORD hath taken away; blessed be the name of the LORD." I so want to have this type of surrender when going through the hard trials in my own life.

Another one of my favorite people in the Bible is Joseph, who was betrayed and sold into slavery by his older brothers while in his youth. He went from the love and comfort of his father's house to being a servant with a master in Egypt. From there, he went into prison for being falsely accused by his master's wife. For years he patiently endured these cruel trials, waiting on God's providence to release him. Each time I read this story, I reflect upon my own ability to endure conflicts that are not as severe as his, and I pray that I will be able to trust the Lord as he did.

My last example is Noah. Noah also had great patience if you really consider his life. Not only did he preach the same message for 120 years—this is patience and endurance—but he also waited for seven days for the Lord to close the door of the ark and over a year for God to open the door back up (see Genesis 7:10; 8:13, 14 KJV). I was once on a cruise for seven days. For me, being on the water was like torture after the first four days. I could hardly wait to be back on dry land. I know many people love cruises, but I am not a huge fan. I often thought of Noah and his family on a boat for all those months. Indeed, that must have been a trying time for all aboard. I'm sure they longed for dry land, and yet, when they saw it, they did not go ahead of the Lord; they waited on Him until His appointed time to open the door (see Psalm 27:14; Isaiah 40:31; Ecclesiastes 3:1; Habakkuk 2:3 KJV). I desire this same patience.

Patience summary. "Patience, my child; in time the grass becomes milk!" is a saying I learned in my childhood. I have contemplated its meaning many times, and it has helped me through many drawn-out processes that I have thirsted to finish. I wanted to drink the milk at the end of the converting process long before the process was done. Indeed, life for all of us has those very trying days. In those days we look at our own profession of faith to see if it's genuine. We must reflect on how we embody patience during these times. Do we bow before our Maker and calmly and cheerfully surrender our trials to Him? In impatience, do we try to solve them in our own human strength, while professing faith? Do we have a calm assurance of His promises? Let's continue to daily self-examine our thoughts, habits, and actions and develop the patience we need to be among God's people in these ending times.

Endurance

Endurance is a word often attached to exercise and stamina. Anything hard takes endurance. Though endurance and patience highly complement one another, endurance differs from patience, being based upon energy and high spirits. Endurance is in one word "power" or "strength."

If we understand the physical laws that govern the body, we will always have physical endurance. In any health crisis, many understand that the power of the immune system is the Eight Laws of Health, which include eating a proper diet free from any dead or diseased animal, getting lots of pure air, getting exposed to plenty of sunlight, drinking and using lots of pure water, exercising daily, enjoying plenty of rest in mind, body, and spirit, abstaining from anything harmful, and trusting in divine power or God's ability to keep His promises! If we adhere to these powerful principles, we will have the power of health to endure any crisis of disease.

Now, having a strong and powerful body is not enough to keep us on our Christian walk. We must also have a powerful spiritual life. Most Christians would tell you that it takes a great deal of fortitude to make it through the Christian walk, but we don't count on our simple human strength. We must walk in the strength of the Almighty, or we are destined to fail.

Biblical examples of endurance. My two fitting biblical examples of endurance in the Old Testament are Jacob and Moses. I will begin with Jacob. Jacob fled from his own country after deceitfully receiving the promised birthright. With the promise of God in a night's dream at Bethel, he journeyed on and endured years of trials in a strange country until returning home. He worked seven years for Rachel, his true love—twice! Though his word upheld the bond for the second seven years, what endurance he gained in that trial! He gained endurance not only in the years of labor for Laban, but also in the agony of having two wives. Those men who think it a glamorous thing to have multiple wives would learn a lesson by reading the life of Jacob.

Being betrayed and cheated by Laban, his father-in-law, must also have been tough for Jacob to endure, especially through that second seven years. But nowhere in his historical record do I read that he lost his temper with Laban, but treated him, a veritable enemy, with love and deference. His character was built by his trials to the point that at Peniel he endured the wrestling match, clinging as with a tight grip to the neck of Christ, which resulted in his name being changed to Israel, meaning overcomer (see Genesis 32:27–30 KJV). Though Jacob's trials continued through the actions of his children for most of his life thereafter, he always had that perfect surrender that helped him endure. He is definitely one of my favorites to think upon when I am in the midst of a trial. May I endure as he did when wronged and treat the wrongdoer with love.

Now, turning to Moses as another great Bible example of endurance from the Old Testament, the Bible says that "he endured, as seeing him who is invisible" (Hebrews 11:27 KJV). When I meditate upon the life of Moses, I begin with those whom the Lord chose to be his parents, Amram and Jochebed. Moses inherited his endurance from them. They not only trusted in the Lord to hide their son as a baby, but once Pharaoh's daughter adopted him as her son, his mother, as his nurse, also taught him to worship the true God. If you truly think on this, this could not have been easy to do. It took both endurance and prayer. I often think of the rigor with which she must have catechized Moses until he was sent to live in the palace.

Moses sensed his life's mission, but because of the Egyptian training he received until the age of forty, he had once more to endure the simple education of the Lord in pastoring the flock of his father-in-law, Jethro, in a strange land (see Exodus 2:22 KJV). It's astounding when you think of the humility Moses acquired through this time. He was once a ruler in Egypt, but he humbled himself to care for the flock of a priest of Midian (see Exodus 2:15; 3:1 KJV). He humbled himself in the sight of the Lord, and the Lord lifted Moses up (see James 4:10 KJV)! The forty years of unlearning the ways of Egypt and learning the ways of the Lord were crucial years in training to care for a flock of people.

Even after enduring the ten plagues that fell upon Egypt, Moses had to endure the journeyings in the wilderness with people whose hearts were bent upon disbelief. Imagine seeing so many signs and wonders and still not believing in the Lord (see Hebrews 3:1–19; 4:2, 6, 11 KJV)! This was pretty much the greatest trial that Moses went through in his lifetime. We know that he became impatient by striking the rock at Meribah twice (see Numbers 20:7–13 KJV). But we also know that he repented and never sinned again after being forgiven. He trusted so much in God that though he was heartbroken because God kept him back from crossing over to Canaan, he faithfully obeyed, trusting in God's will and way.

For his endurance and trust, God raised him up shortly thereafter and took him to the better Canaan in heaven. We know this because he later appeared with Elijah on the Mount of Transfiguration to strengthen Christ for His great trial of Calvary ahead (see Matthew 17:1–8 KJV).

In the Bible, Moses is a type of Christ is linked with Him. There are only four human beings mentioned by name in the Bible who went to heaven. Enoch and Elijah ascended without tasting death (see 2 Kings 2:1–12; Genesis 5:24; Hebrews 11:5 KJV). Moses and Christ tasted death before ascending to heaven, Christ being the divine Victor to conquer death for all who believe upon Him (see Jude 9; John 3:14, 15; Matthew 17:2–5; Hebrews 2:14, 15 KJV). I pray that I endure until the end as did Moses, even if God choses to keep me back from the things I most desire on this toilsome journey to heaven. There is blissful rest for the saints who endure until the end, and I truly strive to be among them.

Endurance summary. I enjoy the saying, "The night is not forever." It is tied to Psalm 30:5 KJV, which states, "Weeping may endure for a night, but joy cometh in the morning." This Scripture gives me strength to press on! Endurance is therefore the power, or strength, to make it through long, tiresome difficulties. This is not *our* strength or power but comes from a higher source.

We all go through times of trial. These delays are often for self-examination, and our continued trust in God is critical. Of ourselves, we can do nothing, but God is the strength of our lives (see John 15:5; Psalm 27:1 KJV). In these times, we may meditate upon the example of Christ—who showcased the ultimate endurance—and upon other biblical examples to whom we are most drawn, to see how they endured. We must also know and remember the promises that are tied to endurance. Look these up in your Bible concordance and commit them to memory. Nothing is more important than to keep our minds upon the Lord. We can endure only if our thoughts remain upon God's strength to conquer all in times of trial. My favorite is Isaiah 40:18–31 KJV. Read it and commit it to memory, as one biblical weapon against fainting in times of trial.

Prayer

Prayer is always intercessory, meaning that no one prays directly to the Father. All prayer is to be addressed to God the Father through His Son, Jesus. Jesus related, "No man cometh unto the Father, but by me" (John 14:6 KJV). He asked us to address the heavenly

Father when He gave us the example of how to pray (see Matthew 6:9 KJV). In the heavenly sanctuary, Jesus is still making intercession for us at the right hand of the Father (see Hebrews 7:25 KJV). We must also be thankful that the entire Godhead is instrumental in our prayers, because even the Holy Ghost also intercedes in our prayers when we do not have the right words to say (see Romans 8:26 KJV).

Because prayer is intercessory above, it must also be intercessory here below. Jesus said, "Thy will be done in earth, as it is in heaven" (Matthew 6:10 KJV). Though we must lift our petitions before God for our needs, we are our brother's keeper. We must daily petition the Throne of Grace for others who are in need of the grace of salvation. The pronouns "our" and "we" are not frivolously placed throughout the Lord's Prayer; they are there because we have a duty to love our fellow man as we love ourselves (See Matthew 6:9–13; John 13:34 KJV).

Many do not know how to pray, supposing it is something that comes easily. However, there is a science to prayer. This science is that we ask, believe, and then graciously receive. It is a simple science, because even a little child may grasp it, but there are many who use words without the faith of believing and never receive! We must remember that God can never be fooled. We must obey His conditions to have our prayers answered.

One condition is to ask in faith, letting go of all doubt (see James 1:6–8 KJV). Doubt is the tool of Satan; faith is a gift of the Spirit (see Galatians 5:22 KJV). We can be trained to doubt just as we can be trained to have faith. For instance, many secular institutions of higher learning require students to take a general education philosophy course. I took philosophy and remember students being truly afraid to express a belief in God for their grade's sake. However, believing the words of any philosopher was accepted. This produces doubt, but not only from the discussions within the philosophy course, but also from the science courses, where the primary textbooks uphold the theory of evolution above how the Bible says all things were created. After taking various courses inferring that God does not truly exist, many unsuspecting students are prone to doubt the existence of God by the time of graduation.

Doubt is not the only thing learned; faith is also learned. Reading and studying the Word of God erases that doubt because "Faith cometh by hearing, and hearing by the word of God" (Romans 10:17 KJV). Just as we grow prone to doubt by repeatedly hearing words that lead us to doubt, so we acquire faith by hearing words that inspire faith.

If we feed our minds with doubt, doubt will grow, but if we feed our minds with faith in the promises of God's Word, faith will grow. If we have faith as a grain of mustard seed, we can grow it until it is strong enough to move mountains (see Matthew 17:20 KJV). Remember, the mustard seed grows into a great tree, and so, our faith can spring up greater than we ever imagined if we let go of doubt and prayerfully study God's Holy Word with the aid of the Spirit of Truth. (See Matthew 13:31, 32; John 16:13 KJV).

To believe in God and His promises is yet another condition. A person who doubts will never even trust his own prayers. Without belief, prayers are mere form, because an answer is never truly expected. If an answer comes, the one who doubts counts it as luck, just as if that person gambled and hit the jackpot. This is not a faith that truly takes hold of God's promises. There's a critical passage concerning faith and doubt written in the book of James that I referenced earlier. James 1:6–8 KJV states: "But let him [the person praying] ask in faith, nothing wavering. For he that wavereth is like a wave of the sea driven with the wind and tossed. For let not that man think that he shall receive any thing of the Lord. A double minded man is unstable in all his ways."

Let's understand this passage by a true-to-life scenario. Imagine a doubting person wanting God to forgive his sins. A well-known promise is, "If we confess our sins, he is faithful and just to forgive us our sins, and to cleanse us from all unrighteousness" (1 John 1:9 KJV). So, yet another condition is to confess our sins. The doubting person confesses his sins in prayer but may be questioning at this point. The Scripture calls that person unstable because he doubts that God would really forgive his sins. Is all lost to those who doubt?

What if a person truly wants to believe but is prone to doubt his prayers? Another well-known promise is, "For God so loved the world, that he gave his only begotten Son, that whosoever *believeth* in him should not perish, but have everlasting life" (John 3:16 KJV). The condition specified is belief, highlighted earlier. Belief is essential to the transaction of forgiveness (see Hebrews 11:6 KJV). However, if the person reaches out with the intent to believe, as did the father of the demoniac child in Mark 9:24 KJV who cried, "Lord, I believe; help thou mine unbelief," God will hear the cry of his heart and reinforce faith. This father saw his need. He saw his true condition, being wretched, miserable, poor, blind, and naked (see Revelation 3:17, 18 KJV). Therefore, the very first thing a sinner must do is to see the need of a Savior.

One sure way to believe that God will answer our prayers is to pray His words (promises, prayers) back to Him. Many prayers are found in the Psalms, but there are many precious promises all throughout the Bible. Take these words as your own. None of God's words come back to Him void, and He hastily performs His words (see Isaiah 55:11; Jeremiah 1:12 KJV). There can be no doubt when praying God's promises, for God always tells the truth; therefore, all His words are sure (see Numbers 23:19; Titus 1:2; Hebrews 6:18 KJV)!

Once we grow in faith by reading the words of God and praying His promises, we will be confident that our prayers will be answered. As we ask God, as did the disciples, to "increase our faith" (Luke 17:5 KJV), He will. This will lead us to claim and receive God's blessings that He is more than willing to bestow upon us. We must always expect an answer to our prayers though it tarry long (see Habakkuk 2:3 KJV). The heartfelt prayer of a righteous person is effectual (see James 5:16 KJV). This means that sure results will spring from our prayers if we fulfill the conditions of right doing, which is righteousness (see 1 John 3:7 KJV).

Most people get stumped when God delays an answer. The tarrying time does not feel safe. In this time, most people lose hope and go to witches, wizards, or psychics because they desire answers. There are warnings in God's Word to stay away from these mediums and trust only in the Almighty God (see

Deuteronomy 18:10–12; Leviticus 19:31; Revelation 21:8 KJV). The waiting is for your good (see Psalm 27:14 KJV). During these times, self-examination is a must. Have seasons of fasting and prayer. God does not hold back any good thing from those who walk uprightly (see Psalm 84:11 KJV). With faith in the Lord, boulders will be removed and nothing will be impossible to those who love the Lord (see Matthew 17:20 KJV)!

Biblical example of prayer. One example of how we must pray comes from Elijah in the Old Testament. Elijah was a man of prayer. He prayed and God did not send rain for the space of three and a half years because of the gross apostasy happening in Israel. This apostasy, generated through an apostate union between King Ahab and Jezebel, caused God's true prophets to be persecuted, many of them put to death. This account is rather equivalent to this our day, where an apostate church union is forming to persecute God's commandment-keeping people.

The showdown upon Mount Carmel was a representation of what true prayer should be. There was a stark contrast between the prayers of those who doubted the God of heaven and the one who believed the words of God. The prophets of Baal and the groves were dancing, shouting, and cutting themselves from morning until evening, but their god(s) never heard them. No fire came to consume the sacrifice they presented. The prophets had repeated phrases such as, "O Baal, hear us!" again and again, but he did not have hearing ears (1 Kings 18:26 KJV). When thinking of how this chapter translates to our day, many of those who doubt the true God of heaven use many words and repetitions to get Him to answer them, but these words are useless when the heart is in doubt.

On the other hand, when it was Elijah's turn to call upon the true God, his manner was so confident that God would answer by fire that he had them flood the altar, the sacrifice, and the trench with water *three times.* Kneeling down, he prayed one simple prayer of confidence in the word of the Lord, and the Lord speedily answered Elijah's petition and sent down fire to burn up the sacrifice and the altar, and to dry up the water in the trench. There was no doubt that the "the LORD, he is the God" (1 Kings 18:39 KJV) and that He hears the prayers of those who confess and forsake their sin.

Later, in the time of King Ahaziah, son of Ahab and Jezebel, the Lord sent the king some unwelcoming news through the prophet Elijah because the king had sought out Baalzebub, instead of the true God, while sick. Consequently, for this sin, the judgment that he would surely die was pronounced against him. Instead of repenting and turning to the Lord, the king proceeded to send three captains of fifty soldiers to get Elijah (see 2 Kings 1:9–14 KJV). Two of these captains and their fifties were consumed by fire, but the third captain humbled himself and interceded for his life and the life of his men. Nowhere in the story do I read that God instructed Elijah to destroy these men, but having the promise of God to rain fire out of heaven once was all the prophet needed to act upon the word of God. He was given this word to claim in 1 Kings 18:24 KJV but used it all those years later in 2 Kings 1 KJV. The word of the Lord stands forever, and we may claim this word again and again (see Isaiah 40:8; 1 Peter 1:25 KJV)!

As I pondered upon this account of Elijah taking the word that God said and using it with confidence in the time of both Ahab and his son Ahaziah, I wondered why we do not take His precious promises and repeat them with confidence as His very words today. There is no other answer than disbelief. Well, I am purposing in my heart to believe, and God has lined up many events to prove this purpose. May I, as well as you reading this, as did Elijah, take the word of God and believe it today, tomorrow, and for years to come (see Hebrews 13:8 KJV).

How to pray. I am yet growing in the science of prayer. As you may have done, I prayed a version of the same prayer again and again. I felt my whole life open up when I understood that Scripture is basically three things: a prayer, a promise, and an instruction. We may pray each of these. How glorious! Starting with the Psalms (and then make your way through the other books of the Bible), find a scripture that encapsulates how you are feeling as you go through a personal experience, and pray that scripture. If that particular scripture is a prayer, pray it. If it is a promise, claim it in prayer. If it is an instruction, ask that God will help you carry it out in your life. Adhering to this will change the way you pray forever.

For example, if I feel I need deliverance when I awake one morning, I go to my Bible concordance and find as many scriptures as I need to pray that relate the key words "deliver, deliverance, help, etc." Psalm 59 KJV is a personal favorite. You can take the whole chapter and read it in a voice just above a whisper to God. You can lead into the prayer saying, "Lord, I am in need of deliverance [in whatever particular area of your life]," and then read as much of that chapter to the Lord as you desire. You may couple scripture prayers together. You don't have to pray just one scripture prayer for deliverance. You can also pray Psalm 116:4 KJV. Add a promise to the prayer of Psalm 116:6 KJV. The scripture of Psalm 50:15 KJV contains two instructions and a promise. Claim the promise and ask God for the strength to know how to carry out the two instructions.

Following this plan, you will daily begin to store up promises in your heart that will enable you to pray more effectively and live for God, carrying out the instructions that are written in His Word. God's Word cannot fail. None of His words come back to Him void (see Isaiah 55:11 KJV). The words He puts into your mouth, He will not only perform, but hasten to perform them (see Jeremiah 1:9, 12 KJV)! However, none of this is possible without belief (see Hebrews 11:6 KJV).

Prayer summary. The best person to call upon in times of need is the Lord (see Hebrews 4:16 KJV). While calling upon Him, we must adhere to the science of prayer, which is to ask, believe, and receive. The best way to ask is to use the scripture prayers, promises, and instructions, as God's words are sure forever. We must wait upon His will and His way. We must ever remember that the Lord made heaven and earth and that there is nothing too hard for Him (see Psalm 121:2; Genesis 18:14; Jeremiah 32:17, 27 KJV). In prayer, we can cast all our care upon Him, for He cares for us and will supply our every need if we never doubt (see 1 Peter 5:7; Philippians 4:19 KJV).

Conclusion

The energy to maintain a Christian life comes from patience, endurance, and prayer. Each of these entails the attitude, strength, and faithful trust we must daily exhibit in Christ, and even on account of Christ. Of ourselves, we can do nothing, but Christ working in us helps us along (see John 15:5; Philippians 2:13 KJV).

Christ is our ultimate example, revealing a perfect life with P.E.P. in His steps. As we daily imbibe His words, His Spirit will shine in our hearts and reveal a life that can withstand any trial. He said, "I have overcome the world" (John 16:33 KJV). Because He is an overcomer, we are all overcomers. All we must do is bear His likeness, surrendering ourselves upon the cross He chooses for us daily (see 2 Corinthians 3:18; 1 Corinthians 15:31 KJV).

As we surrender, we will gain the experience needed to withstand the trials of the coming crisis, because as we were being tried and proved in the past, we used the godly P.E.P. with a song to come forth as gold (see Job 23:10 KJV). Our desires and our mind will be one with His mind (see Philippians 2:5 KJV). When answers tarry or trials seem long, we will not faint but hold on to Him in patience, for patience is a characteristic of the enduring saints (see Revelation 14:12 KJV). So, I pray that we let patience do her "perfect work" and that we are led to endure with a life of prayer (see James 1:4 KJV). The promise is that they who "endure unto the end, the same shall be saved" (Matthew 24:13 KJV). I therefore pray we endure! Indeed, may God bless all reading these words to endure until the end!

THE IMPORTANCE OF A MARK!
Brief Bible Prophecy

" "

Behold, he cometh with clouds; and every eye shall see him,
and they also which pierced him: and all kindreds of the
earth shall wail because of him. Even so, Amen.
REVELATION 1:7 KJV

Christ is coming! I say this daily because I believe it is near, based upon the signs that are fast fulfilling from God's Holy Word. We are commanded by Christ to watch (see Matthew 24:42 KJV). Many do not believe it because there has been a tarrying time. In this section—though only the Holy Spirit can convince you at the end of this discussion—I want to briefly lay out the biblical facts that we are living in the end of time and to relate the signs and prophetic fulfillment that show Christ's coming is very near. I pray that this discussion at least gets you looking deeper into a larger study of all that now constitutes the present truth of the glorious Second Advent.

The Signs

Biblical signs are now in the land, and many people may see these signs as normal. Indeed, wars and rumors of wars, pestilence, famines, and earthquakes, or calamities, in various places have occurred in the past, but there is something peculiar regarding the way these are occurring today (see Matthew 24:3, 6, 7; Mark 13:4, 7, 8; Luke 21:7, 9–11 KJV). Extraordinarily, these signs are now occurring simultaneously and frequently. The rate and compounded occurrence of these should cause the thinking person to ponder what the Bible says will take place in the last days.

Now, prophetically, these signs will lead people living in these times to think on God and seek out a spiritual solution. This seemingly religious solution will bring on a state of things that will cause this world to end. Indeed, many solutions will lead up to a final one. These "solutions" will be compulsory to our individual conscience to serve the Lord. This means there will be penalties for not following these solutions, but God tells us plainly in His Word that we ought to obey Him and not any man-made law going against His Word (see Acts 5:29 KJV).

Coupled with these major signs of the last days is the disease in the animal kingdom, which will affect the health of all still consuming animal products—even by-products. If you have never considered a plant-based diet, it is to be considered now. Hosea 4:1–4 KJV relates that the land and the beasts, even the marine life, will languish, or be diseased. It is for us to truly decide to give these things up, if we desire to be healthy.

There is a great deal of amalgamation happening with the foods. Genetically modified foods (GMO) are making it harder and harder to eat completely natural produce. We must get hold of organic seeds and sow our own gardens. This is not a suggestion, but a reality if we are not looking to compromise our health. Now, if you are not able to do this, please do not lose hope. God is acquainted with our situations and is able to cause the foods He gave us at Creation Week sustain us through this end-time period. The Bible says plainly that whatever we eat or drink, we must do it to the glory of God, which means we must pray over everything we ingest, as God alone can make it pure (see 1 Corinthians 10:31 KJV).

I am aware that I cannot do justice to end-time prophecy in a brief discussion, but I really want to hit the highlights. I want to discuss the major end-time prophecy to open eyes to what is about to happen as we see these signs converging. There will be a leader who is in the background pulling strings, but most of us will be able to see only the puppet actors, who may not know what is particularly occurring. From here, a major, final crisis will hit called the Mark of the Beast, but first we must know who the Beast is in order to understand what this mark is.

The Beast

In the Bible a beast means a king or kingdom (see Daniel 7:19, 23 KJV). The fourth beast in Daniel is pagan Rome, which became papal Rome at the introduction of the little horn (see Daniel 7:24, 8; 8:9 KJV). Daniel is the prophetic book that unlocks or reveals Revelation. Thus, the beast in Revelation 13:1–10 KJV is the Roman Catholic Church, or the papacy, which ruled the earth for 1,260 years (see Daniel 7:25; Revelation 12:14, 6 KJV).

The papacy has two primary designations. One is as a political power (the beast) and the other as a church power (Mystery

Babylon the Great, as discussed in Revelation 17:1–5 KJV). The combination of church and state is significant in prophecy, as it counterfeits the theocracy set up by God in the Old Testament. When Jerusalem was destroyed, no other theocracy was to again be in this earth until the Second Coming of Christ, when all things shall be new and there will be a New Jerusalem. But this, like many of God's designs, has been counterfeited by the papacy. The difference is the compulsory nature of the counterfeit government. God's government, even in the human heart, is not one of compulsion but of love.

During the 1,260 years, the Roman Catholic Church ruled the kingdoms and nations. She allowed no free thought to threaten her power. Even the rarest Bibles were destroyed once translated into the people's tongue. She held supreme authority politically and spiritually.

Even today, the Roman Catholic Church claims to be the "Mother Church" of all Christian denominations. In that sense, she is the woman with whom the kings of the earth commit fornication in Revelation 17:2 KJV. Throughout the Bible, a woman is likened unto a church, and this understanding unlocks Bible prophecy (see Jeremiah 6:2; Ephesians 5:25–27; 2 Corinthians 11:2 KJV). The deeper this is studied, the clearer the end time Bible prophecy becomes. I pray that after reading the brief overview in this book, you will look further into this, especially via the suggested resources—such as *The Great Controversy*—in the back of this book.

During this time of supreme papal authority in matters of both church and state, the papacy made war against any and all who dared to question her authority. This was the Old World in which no dissenter of her papal authority was tolerated, not even the kings of the nations. Many who upheld freedom of conscience were either put in prison, exiled, or put to death. This fierce and strange-looking beast had never been seen before as a ruling power. Force was her method of causing acquiescence.

During this time, the Roman Catholic Church changed the seventh-day Sabbath to a first-day memorial of Christ's death, not based upon any biblical authority, but because she reigned supreme. This is a historical fact that cannot be refuted! The Bible in Daniel 7:25 KJV states that she (the church) would think to change times (meaning the days of the week) and laws (meaning God's Ten Commandments, especially the Fourth Commandment, which she changed to the third and totally did away with the second Commandment, forbidding any to worship idols).

Nearing the end of the 1,260 years of papal domination, all who could flee from the iron teeth of her authority fled to the New World, under a more liberal or lamblike system of government, promoting civil government and religious freedom (see Revelation 13:11 KJV). The crafters of the United States Constitution put in checks to never again allow a church and state government, but those protections would last only so long. We are entering the period where this same government will speak as a dragon by forming an image to the papal beast!

The Image of the Beast

The lamblike beast that arose out of the earth and formed the image to the beast in Revelation 13:11–17 KJV is apostate Protestant America. This image is an apostate because America was founded by Protestants fleeing papal rule in Europe. These Protestants have been infiltrated by the Roman Catholic Jesuits, whose main mission is to overthrow Protestantism and revive popery. The first step is already done: Protestantism as we knew it was legally signed away on October 31, 2017. Thus, the image to the beast will mirror the Old World Order that the Papacy established in the Dark Ages in what is to be called the New World Order.

This can be done very easily. First, the Sunday Blue Laws—which I refer to as "Billy Blue" in my poem entitled "Second Advent: End-time Messages"—are still on the books in most states. Secondly, the currency must change to be easily controlled by the existing powers, and thus, digital currency is making its way swiftly into the economic realm. Thirdly, intelligence data must exist for every human being in the global world. Movements must be easily tracked. Today, we are living in an era in which tracking data is prized under the auspices of quality assessments. Our parents and their parents lived quality lives without these intrusive quality assessments.

I pray that even those who are longing for a religious revival in America and who advocate folks attending Sunday worship services by law will understand that just because they agree with this law does not make it a fair law. Anything that forces the conscience is not freedom to choose. If God made us free to make a choice to serve Him, we should not take that right away from any individual. It is a truly inalienable right! One friend with whom I went to college affirmed that she would love such a law, but to her I repeat a quote that I can attribute only to my late supervisor Dr. Thomas E. H. Conway, Jr. because I do not know if it originated with him: "No freedom for one means no freedom for all." Indeed!

The Sabbath

In Genesis 2:1–3 KJV, we see that God rested on the Sabbath from the work He did in the first week of Creation. Yes, it is written that God rested on the Sabbath. What is good for God must be good for us! He made the Sabbath a holy day of rest. He sanctified it, causing it to be set apart for holy use. This is most significant because this rest took place upon the seventh day of the week—the day that ended the week.

"God rested on the Sabbath. What's good for God must be good for us!"

Today, many rest upon the first day of the week. Unlike the seventh day of the week, which has its biblical authority laid in its foundation at the ending of Creation Week and within the Ten Commandments, the first day is never given any hallowing authority in all of Scripture. Do your best to find it; it is simply not there.

The logical question arises as to why the majority of the Christian world keeps Sunday, the first day of the week, as the Sabbath. Well, it is grounded in papal tradition, beginning on March 7, 321 A.D. Constantine, the emperor of Rome, declared

Sunday to be a holy day by law as a political compromise to unite his subjects, which were both pagans and Christians. He claimed to have had a vision where he saw a cross in the sun and heard a command to conquer using the sign of the cross. As time went on, more and more creeping compromises were found among the churches until they finally pressed down the seventh-day Sabbath of the Bible for the first-day Sabbath of the Roman Catholic Church.

Even today, the Roman Catholic Church in *The Convert's Catechism of Catholic Doctrine* relates that she has changed the Sabbath to Sunday (see the section regarding the Third Commandment, which is really the Fourth Commandment. You see, she appears to get a kick out of changing things that God set up). By her authority the Sabbath has been changed, hearkening back to the prophetic change of times and laws in Daniel 7:25 KJV. So, today it may be truly tradition that keeps this intelligent and informed generation hallowing Sunday. They do it because their parents and grandparents did it, and so on and so forth. Perhaps they may be ignorant of the true Sabbath, which is one reason this discussion is part of this book. In the time of ignorance, God winks, but once light comes, so must obedience (see Acts 17:30 KJV).

The seventh-day Sabbath was to be observed by the whole world as a sign, or seal, of God's redemptive power (see Ezekiel 20:12, 20 KJV). It is the seal of God as verily as any earthly monarch has a seal. A seal bears the name, title, territory of a ruler (see Esther 3:12 KJV). God's seal is in His law, His Ten Commandments. Specifically, his seal resides in the Fourth Commandment (see Isaiah 8:16; Exodus 20:3–17; 20:8–11 KJV).

The Fourth Commandment is the longest of all the Ten Commandments, and it shows us exactly God's name, title, and territory, just like an earthly seal. This commandment specifies God's name as "Lord," His title as "Maker," and His territory as "heaven and earth" (Exodus 20:11 KJV). It really is just that plain!

It gets even plainer too! The Fourth Commandment reveals that the seventh-day Sabbath is a memorial of Him as our Creator and the Maker of heaven and earth. This is important because certain people say that the Sabbath was given just for the Jews; however, all one has to do is go to Genesis 2:1–3 to see that it was instituted hundreds of years before the first Jew existed. We also know that in the Fourth Commandment, God calls us to "remember" the Sabbath was instituted at Creation. This is strong evidence that it was not made for only the Jews. God made the Sabbath for all mankind (see Mark 2:27 KJV).

During Israel's many years in bondage, they forgot the sacred institution of the Sabbath and needed reminder, a call to worship. But the Sabbath was not only for them, when God wrote the Ten Commandments with His own divine finger. The Fourth Commandment also stated that "thy stranger (meaning someone who was not a Jew) that is within thy gates" must also keep the seventh-day Sabbath (Exodus 20:10 KJV). Here is more unmistakable evidence that the seventh-day Sabbath was for everyone. This evidence is backed up by more scriptures in the Old Testament. According to the Bible there should always be two or three witnesses to establish a truth (see Deuteronomy 19:15; Matthew 18:16; 2 Corinthians 13:1 KJV). Therefore, read the following scriptures in your King James Version Bible connecting the word "stranger" with the seventh-day the Sabbath of the Lord: Deuteronomy 5:14; Isaiah 56:6 KJV.

In the Old Testament, we see that God calls the seventh-day Sabbath "my holy day." And He commands all desirous of receiving the heritage of Jacob—which is the Promised Land or Canaan, the spiritual heritage pointing to heaven and the earth made new—to delight in the Sabbath (see Isaiah 58:13, 14 KJV). We also see that the seventh-day Sabbath will be kept in heaven (see Isaiah 66:22, 23 KJV). It does not just say the Jews in these verses, but "all flesh." This means everyone. I am not a Jew by ethnicity, and I definitely want to be included in that number. I am so thankful that I am a member of "all flesh!"

In the New Testament, the seventh-day Sabbath did not change. There are no instances of an authoritative change by Christ while on earth or by His commandment to the apostles to worship on another day. Hebrews 4:8 KJV states, "For if Jesus had given them rest, then would he not afterward have spoken of another day." Indeed, He did not! The God I serve is not slack. He is not forgetful either. There would be no question of His change. Just as He plainly instituted the Communion and foot washings before His death, He would have plainly told us to observe Sunday.

Many people call themselves New Testament Christians, not realizing that the New Testament confirms the seventh-day Sabbath in greater power than the Old Testament. It is within the New Testament that we see Jesus keeping the seventh-day Sabbath, preaching and teaching (see Mark 6:2; Luke 4:16, 31; 6:6; 13:10 KJV). It is within the New Testament that we see Him calling

Himself Lord of the Sabbath and indicating that the Sabbath was not specifically made for the Jews but for man (See Matthew 12:8; Mark 2:27, 28; Luke 6:5 KJV). It is the New Testament where we see the Sabbath released from man's oppressive laws. It is lawful to do well upon the Sabbath (see Matthew 12:12 KJV). We may show compassion to others on the Sabbath (see Matthew 12:2, 11; Mark 2:24–26; 3:2–5; Luke 6:2, 7–10; 13:14–16; 14:3, 5; John 5:8–10, 16, 18; 7:23; 9:14 KJV). It is the New Testament that shows Jesus *resting* upon the Sabbath, even in His death (see Matthew 27:62–66; 28:1; Mark 15:42-46; 16:1, 2; Luke 23:54–56 KJV). It is the New Testament that reveals that the apostles kept the Sabbath (see Acts 13:14, 42–44; 16:13; 17:2; 18:4; 1 Corinthians 11:1; Revelation 1:10 KJV). Lastly, it is the New Testament that reveals the Gentile converts also keeping the Sabbath according to the still binding Ten Commandments (see Acts 13:44–52; 17:1–4; 18:4 KJV).

There was never any change to the Sabbath in the New Testament, but on the contrary, the Sabbath was upheld as God's holy day (see Hebrews 4:4, 10 KJV). In Hebrews 4:11 KJV, the Bible tells us to work to enter into *that* rest, which is the specific rest, the seventh-day rest, God took at Creation. It reveals that this rest *still* remains (see Hebrews 4:9 KJV). Compounded with this remaining rest is the fact that God Himself does not change. He is the same "yesterday, and to day, and for ever" (Hebrews 13:8 KJV). In relation to the end times, Jesus tells us to pray that our flight not be on the Sabbath (see Matthew 24:20 KJV). Thus, we can see that He will care that we observe the Sabbath even during our time of persecution and flight. Indeed, our only duty is to fear, obediently worship, Him and keep His commandments (see Ecclesiastes 12:13 KJV). I pray that we all obey Him, desiring to keep His seventh-day Sabbath out of love for our Creator!

The Mark of the Beast

Now that we have briefly identified the Beast, and the Image of the Beast, and revealed the Sabbath to be the seal (or sign or mark) of God's creative and redemptive power, we are now ready to identify the Mark of the Beast. The Mark of the Beast is the seal of *man 's* creative power. This was specified in Daniel 7:25 KJV, where it states that the Beast would think to change times and laws. The only times and laws now changed is the seventh-day Sabbath. It is a time as it is the seventh day of the week. It is a law because it is the fourth precept of God's holy Law, which stands forever (see Isaiah 40:8; 1 Peter 1:25 KJV). God's Ten Commandments are His very words written with His own finger, declaring these ten precepts are forever (see Deuteronomy 9:10; Exodus 31:18; Malachi 3:6; Hebrews 13:8 KJV). Thus, it has to be this law that was changed in order to fulfill the prophecy of the times and laws in Daniel.

As we have already seen, the Roman Catholic Church admits in her *Convert's Catechism* that she changed the Sabbath to Sunday. The change was made on account of worship. God desires His creation to serve (or worship—see Matthew 4:10 KJV) only Him. The Beast institution, the Roman Catholic Church, desires the exact same homage God desires from His creation. We should obey only the Lord (see Acts 5:29 KJV). Because of this controversy over worship, the Mark of the Beast is *enforced* Sunday worship, as related in Revelation 13 KJV. Yes, enforced or compulsory worship. Sunday worship will not be the Mark until there is a denying of individual rights to choose whom to obey. This is how it was in the Old World, and this is how it will be in the new. In Revelation 13:15–17 KJV, we see the word "worship," and this same word is also cited in Revelation 14:9, 10 regarding the Mark. This worship is directly opposing the true worship called for by the first angel in Revelation 14:6, 7 KJV, where it loudly warns all of creation—"them that dwell on the earth, and to every nation, and kindred, and tongue, and people"—to "worship him that made heaven, and earth, and the sea, and the fountains of waters."

Because the Old World also had compulsory worship, why was that not the Mark of the Beast? Well, the Mark of the Beast is prophesied to come right before the coming of Christ, which is the reaping of the harvest in Revelation 14:14–16 KJV. The harvest is to take place at the time of the end, which begin in 1798. It was prophesied that the Roman Catholic Church would receive total world dominance, which happened under Emperor Justinian, who gave the pope of Rome total control of all the churches in 538 A.D. This control lasted for 1,260 years, being threatened only by the Protestant Reformation of the sixteenth century. Adding the 1,260 years to 538 A.D. results in the year 1798 A.D., when the Roman Catholic Church received a deadly wound from General Louis Berthier, a skilled and trusted commander in Napoleon Bonaparte's army. Berthier kidnapped Pope Pius VI, severely wounding the political and spiritual power of the Vatican (see Daniel 12:1, 2, 7;

Revelation 13:3 KJV). However, after 1798, the deadly wound would be healed in the United States of America (see Revelation 13:11–17 KJV).

The United States will lead the enforcement of the Mark of the Beast. It is already taking steps to do this. This can be best seen in the address the pope gave to Congress in September 2015. Never before in the U.S. was any religious power given the stage to set policy in our legislative halls. Any nation that extols religious dominance will have persecution for dissenters. This was seen with the Puritans, and it will be seen again under the Image to the Beast—apostate Protestant America, which will enforce the Mark of the Beast. Currently, the significant climate and health crises have created opportunities to set a new normal, or to reset, our day-to-day life. These have affected our individual freedoms, and, with the introduction of digital currency, each one of us is at the mercy of the government, which is bowing to the church-state policies of Rome.

The Antichrist

If the Mark of the Beast is compulsory Sunday worship, then the person who authorizes the enforcement of a day contrary to the day the Lord set up for worship must be the antichrist, or the premiere antichrist. There will be many antichrists, but this one specifically refers to the one, the man, mentioned in Revelation 13:18 and 2 Thessalonians 2:3, 4 KJV (see also Matthew 24:22–24; 1 John 2:18 KJV). Among the many, there is the greatest antichrist of all who does everything in his power to change God's law and His precepts. This man is none other than the pope of Rome.

For those saying they do not see the number 666 on the pope, you just have to know where to look. Remember that the sign or seal of God contains His name, title, and territory. This number is also a sure sign of the antichrist. The number then must be embedded in his name, title, or territory. There are a number of ways to get to the 666 number of a man, but one of the best known ways Seventh-day Adventists calculate this number is through his title, "Vicarious Filii Dei." (See Revelation 13:18 KJV). This title is most significant because it relates that the pope claims to be the substitute for, or in the place of, God on earth. This directly fulfills 2 Thessalonians 2:3, 4 KJV—which is blasphemy—and the pope is prophesied to blaspheme God (see John 10:30–33; Mark 2:5–7; Revelation 13:6 KJV). Study the figure for this calculation:

VICARIUS FILII DEI

THE LITERAL MEANING: **Vicarius** → Substituting for, or in place of
                                          Filii → Son
                                          Dei → God

V	=	5		F	=	No value		D	=	500
I	=	1		I	=	1		E	=	No value
C	=	100		L	=	50		I	=	1
A	=	No value		I	=	1				501
R	=	No value		I	=	1				
I	=	1				53				
U/V	=	5								
S	=	No value								
		112								

$$112 + 53 + 501 = 666$$

Figure 1: Historical calculation of the title Vicarius Filii Dei
Source: http://www.666-mark-of-the-beast.info/mark16.php

Conveniently, this title has been reported as retired by Pope Francis; however, God's people know that the Roman Catholic Church never changes, despite her "apologies" for the numerous atrocities she has committed in the past. Further studies in Bible prophecy relate that the Beast has leopard-like spots, which point to it never changing, though she may hide her deeds (see Revelation 13:2; Jeremiah 13:23 KJV). If you had searched online for "Vicarius Filii Dei" even ten years ago, many proofs of this title would have returned, but now the internet is being scrubbed of all that points to the pope as Antichrist. Therefore, already as in the Old World, darkness is falling fast among the population, which indicates a new age of darkness is coming. May all reading this do their best to find truth in the historical records outside of the internet before this fact fades, as the seventh-day Sabbath did from the memory of the majority of the Christian world today.

For those who are reading this and are startled, this information is not new to Protestantism. Protestants have known this all the while, but like the Fourth Commandment, they have forgotten and have become apostates, but God is now calling all of those with true hearts back to Him. I pray you come before it is too late. I pray that we all be the witnesses who bring light to areas of darkness in the world today!

Choice!

Choice is a fundamental individual right. It gives us the freedom to choose the direction of our lives. Force takes freedoms away. This is truly the principle upon which Protestant America was founded. This is what was so attractive to all who desired to emigrate here.

The freedom to live according to the dictates of one's own conscience is prized above money. Thomas Paine is credited with saying, "Give me liberty or give me death!" because no one is truly *living* whose conscience is forced!

We can see the beginnings of a world where individual freedoms are sacrificed for the good of the many. This is what is called Common Good policy, which is a fundamental Roman Catholic doctrine. We have been indoctrinated to see this as a good policy—until it hits home to our individual rights. The saying, "No freedom for one means no freedom for all" is true. No one escapes its depressive power, even if for a time compliance is chosen. Because no one escapes this, there will come a time when all will have to make a choice to worship God or to worship the Beast and his Image and receive his Mark (see Revelation 14:9, 10 KJV). Let's study our Bible and get familiar with its end-time prophecy. Also, a powerful book to read for this time is *The Great Controversy* by Ellen Gould White, which recounts the historical and prophetic events now being fulfilled. May we not be ignorant of what is rapidly occurring on this earth, which will take many who do not read by surprise!

I urge you to remember that blessings and cursings are ingrained in every choice. In every choice there is life and death. Today, I choose to worship God, and I call you to actively choose Him too while you still can (see Deuteronomy 30:19 KJV)! Maranatha!

Suggested Resources

SUGGESTED RESOURCES

ONLINE RESOURCES / MINISTRIES

For books, such as *The Great Controversy, The Ministry of Healing, Steps to Christ*, and many more, see:

The Ellen G. White Estate, Inc.
https://whiteestate.org/

Ellen G. White Writings
https://egwwritings.org/

To purchase these books, you may visit:

Harvestime Books
https:// harvestimebooks.com/

Please visit the following ministries to hear present truth:

Saved to Serve/Prophesy Again Ministry
https:// prophesyagain.org/

Gospel of Health Ministry
https:// gospelofhealth.com

"

Did you know that the Authorized King James Version (KJV) Bible is the one that led the Protestants through the Protestant Reformation? It is the purest inspired Word of God in the English vernacular. It will reveal a harmony of scripture as you study it line upon line and precept upon precept (see Isaiah 28:9, 10 KJV). Prophetic truths will come alive as literal interpretations shine light upon the prophetic. Indeed, the Bible explains itself. May we take no man's word above it! In other versions of the Bible, even the highly regarded and popular New King James Version, many scriptures/words have been changed or even deleted. These modifications have perilous salvific ramifications. This tampering is as dangerous as the Bible burnings during the Dark Ages to remove God's Word from the hands and minds of the people. Please research this for yourself. I pray you will desire the pure Word of God and that this knowledge helps you to make the KJV your study Bible as you study on to know the Lord!

To understand why the Authorized King James Bible is the best modern translation, watch/read:

Dr. Gail Kiplinger: New Age Bible Versions
https:// youtube.com/watch?v=czp47-K5GtE

Bill Hughes: Sun Worship Bible Versions
https:// youtube.com/watch?v=8-Otd_IziiQ

Bonus: In Memoriam of Godly Parents

POEM 58

Losing Our Father!

"

The glory of children are their fathers.
PROVERBS 17:6 KJV

What a loss to lose our father,
A man gentle, firm, but kind—
A man of high respect
And humble intellect,
Who loved God with all his mind!

In the losing of our father,
Our lives must be adjusted.
With our mother's death,
We have been bereft
Of the parents God us entrusted.

A principle man was Daddy;
His faith he held so strong.
One of the last of them
Who were the best of men—
We will miss him all lifelong!

Unpretentious were his actions,
The truth is what he'd choose,
And he was fair to all—
The great and small—
Even when it seemed he'd lose.

His gain is in his legacy.
What an example to us all!
At the trumpet sound
Hoping his starry crown
Will reflect his protocol.

Yes, we hope to see our father
When Christ Jesus comes again.
And His coming's near,
For the signs are clear
And are quickly rushing in!

POEM 59

Our Resurrection Hope

Blessed are the dead which die in the Lord from henceforth:
Yea, saith the Spirit, that they may rest from their labours;
and their works do follow them.
REVELATION 14:13 KJV

Friday morning Mom died—
It broke our hearts
(Her life so well respected),
And we look forward to the day
When she'll be resurrected.

God'll call her forth in perfect health
(Yes, she'll be whole again) —
For this we know, when Christ returns,
He'll rid this world of sin.

We're still in shock or disbelief.
We'll miss her lovely smile,
Her heart of gold, and those loving arms
To hold us for a while.

But if we're faithful to the end,
We'll be with her that day,
For blessed are the dead who die in Christ,
The Truth, the Life, the Way!

Heaven's the place of our reward—
No death will ever be.
There, we'll rejoice without one tear
Around the glassy sea.

POEM 60

Remembering Daddy

" "

And, ye fathers, provoke not your children to wrath: but bring
them up in the nurture and admonition of the Lord.
EPHESIANS 6:4 KJV

To seek those things which are above
Is how Dad lived his life,
Testifying of the Father's love
Within this world of strife.

Before he gave his message
Each Sabbath he would say,
"No greater God could bless us"—
"In the Sanctuary is His Way!"

He believed a life that's hid in Christ
Meant that we would live again
For to die to *self,* surrendering life,
Is gaining victory over sin.

O, tremendously we will miss him
Now that he sleeps in rest!
We have the hope that God will list him
Among the children of the blest.

Please keep us in prayer,
For our ev'ry tear
Is for ourselves that we'll be
More faithful and true
This whole crisis through,
To inherit eternity.

About the Author

BRIEF BIO
Samara Fleming

❝

Whatsoever ye do, do all to the glory of God.
1 CORINTHIANS 10:31 KJV

Samara has been a lover of poetry since childhood, when her mother would give her illustrated Bible stories in rhyme to read. It was only natural for her to begin to write poetry at a young age. Her first epic historical poem was written for an American History class project on the Second Great Awakening during her junior year of high school. From there, her first published Christian poem, "Affirmations of the Unseen," revised in this book, was published near the end of her teenage years. Samara continues to love poetry regarding truth and righteousness. Her main desire is to keep the glory of God in view through her poetic works.

As a devoted Seventh-day Adventist Christian, one of Samara's greatest efforts is dedicated to sharing the present truth for this time. The most prominent way she does this is through her plant-based food blog, Simple Preparations (https://simplepreparations.com), which she launched in 2016 to honor the legacy of her mother. In this blog she relates the spiritual and physical importance of returning to the original diet God gave to man for health of body, mind, and soul, as we are now in a pivotal time of increasing pestilence.

Though Samara is originally a native of Connecticut, she has lived most of her life in the South. She received her baccalaureate, master's, and terminal degrees in the areas of humanities, social sciences, and education from North Carolina State University, where she also served as professional staff for over a decade. Later, Samara taught first-year general education courses at a proprietary college. Currently, she resides in North Carolina along with her two precious and undomesticated felines, Lucy and Cautious.

Lightning Source UK Ltd.
Milton Keynes UK
UKHW041931101122
411987UK00004B/246